CRIME WAVE

BY

ROBERT JAMES CARMACK

www.lulu.com and RJCarmack Publishing

Crime Wave

Copyright © 2012 by Robert James Carmack

October 2012

ISBN 978-1-105-57404-8

Other books by Robert James Carmack:

Protégé

Copyright © 2011 by Robert James Carmack

January 2011

ISBN 978-1-4357-7110-9

Protégé II

Copyright © 2011 by Robert James Carmack

First Edition January 2011

ISBN 978-1-4583-7641-1

Friday June 24, 2011

Akron, Ohio

University of Akron Campus

Detective James Nelson knelt down next to the body of Angela Hart and shook his head slowly. The forty-five year old father of three pushed away the thought that the young University of Akron volleyball player was almost the same age as his own daughter. His partner Beth Woodson walked up while pulling on a pair of latex gloves. She was a twenty-nine year old that had previously served two tours of duty in Afghanistan and was a third generation police officer with the department.

Detective Woodson looked down at her partner, "So far we have no witnesses. What do you have here?"

Nelson replied without looking up, "No ID on her. Another student confirmed her ID as Angela Hart, student athlete and volleyball player on full scholarship."

A scream came from one of the crowd of onlookers. A campus police officer approached the two detectives.

"One of her teammates is here if you want to talk to her?"

James stood up, "I'll speak with her."

Beth Woodson brushed the long hair from the face of the young girl who lay behind some bushes along a path that threaded its way among the campus buildings. Bruises covered her mouth and dried blood was crusted on her lips. Beth estimated the girl to be six-three or four and to weigh a solid one-seventy. She wore a blue "Fear The Roo" athletic department T-shirt and matching sweat pants. She was missing her left shoe. Beth lifted her left foot and examined the back of the heel. The skin was torn and bloody. The back of the right foot was similarly battered above the shoe-line.

An officer called the detective over to the nearest building. The fifteen story dormitory was one of the tallest buildings in this area of the campus and it seemed even taller due to the enormous cell phone tower mounted on its roof. James caught up with Beth just as she was about to enter the building via the rear stairwell.

Tucking his notepad into his back pocket, James smilingly related, "Teammate stated that they regularly use the stairwells here to run up to the top because they are spacious, well lit and quote, make neat echoes when you are running in there."

The two detectives walked the stairs all the way up to the top floor, stopping just short of the door to the roof to examine the last steps where they spotted small blood stains and pieces of skin from the back of the girl's heels. Without a word they opened the door and walked out onto the roof.

The surface of the roof was a white vinyl type of material that was soft and smooth. The lip of the building extended about three feet above the roof and had a fence atop that which went up another five feet. Near the center of the roof was a large rectangular structure and a cell tower sprouting from its center and extending far up into the sky. Black scuff marks covered so many areas of the surface that it would be extremely difficult to determine when or if any of them had belonged to the victim or her attacker.

James spoke up.

"Her teammate also said that they often would come out onto the roof for a walking lap or two for the fresh air and the view."

Beth finally began the process of bouncing ideas off of her partner as they walked the perimeter of the roof.

"So she makes it to the roof and is taking in the view. It is a beautiful view from up here. I think it would be easy to be distracted and not notice someone coming up behind you."

James cut in.

"That girl was six-four and one seventy at least. She was in great shape, going to take one strong son of a bitch to strangle her. We need to talk to any boyfriends, maybe on the track team, football player, weight lifter type."

Woodson nodded while jotting notes and added, "Right and then try to drag her down the stairs.

Probably only tried the dragging down the first flight before picking her up and carrying her down the remaining fourteen flights. You think you could carry me down fourteen flights?"

"I doubt it. So....why go to the trouble? Got more chance of being spotted carrying her down the stairs than if you just leave her up here."

"Unless you want her to be found. Or....if you don't want her to be found up here."

"So what's up here that someone might be hiding or not want to bring attention to?"

They walked the roof again and once more found nothing out of the ordinary. The structure around the cell tower had a single door on it and that was padlocked. The padlock had a wire tie wound through it that would break upon opening and a tag stating that it was last opened three weeks earlier on the first of the month. A sign on the door stated that it was the property of the Akron Police Department.

1975

Akron, Ohio

Eighteen year old Frankie Tarasco sat in his basement hangout for hours playing the hottest games ever, Pong and Tank Battle. The simplistic games fascinated the world as kids had their first chance to play them at home and not in the arcades at the mall.

It wasn't long before he had the cover off and like every other electronic device in the house; he had dismantled it to figure out how it worked.

Frankie had a high school science teacher who introduced him to the world of computers and he was soon hooked. He studied everything he could about them.

1981

Akron, Ohio

Frankie Tarasco now relaxed by zapping the alien space invaders, pulverizing asteroids and nailing centipedes as the game systems began developing more sophistication.

When he wasn't playing games he was learning the basics of computer programming. He soon learned how programming took place and became proficient in one of the many programming languages, COBOL or Common Business Oriented Language.

He bought into the Hacker's ethic which originally believed in improving computer systems using any means. Generally those hackers would work on a system trying to improve it, constantly building upon the work of others who had gone before them. They shared their work without reservation. Part of the ethic dealt with unlocking any doors in the systems and Frankie liked this part particularly well. The one area of the hacker's ethic that Frankie did not care about was that hacking should not be done for personal profit. He had decided that personal profit was the only way to go.

1982
Akron, Ohio
Firestone Park

Frankie Tarasco pulled his caddy up in front of the small tract house and parked on the street. In the passenger seat was the owner of the home, Angelo Martin.

As they walked up the drive the next door neighbor stood waxing his car, he stopped and called out, "Hey Angelo, you look pretty happy."

Angelo beamed as he waved his neighbor over, "I am Tommy. Tommy this is my friend Frankie T.....Frankie, this is my neighbor Tommy Smith."

After everyone had shaken hands, they walked around to the backyard.

"So what's the good news?", Tommy asked as they sat down at a large wooden picnic table.

"Frankie got me in at this new place called Firebrand Electronics up in Cleveland. Making computers and stuff. Gonna be making some good money too."

"Really....hmmm....like how good? If you don't mind my asking?"

"It's like double what I'm making now."

Frankie asked Tommy, "Are you looking for a job too?"

"Well….for more money, I'd be a fool not to keep my eyes open."

It was in this way that the two neighbors became co-workers. Both men had baby boys less than a year old named Mario and Ronnie. As their sons grew up, they became inseparable. Frankie T attended various family outings, backyard barbecues, birthday parties and frequently showed up at the boys sporting events.

Uncle Frankie always remained something of a mystery. No one ever really knew what kind of work he did but he always seemed flush with cash, always seemed to be driving a new sports car and would drop in after being gone for long periods of time.

1992

Frankie spent the better part of two years trying to enter into the banking system of a local institution before hitting pay dirt. Once in, he was able to create phony savings accounts and then credit them with amounts varying from twenty to forty thousand dollars each.

He soon had two accomplices begin entering the banks various branches and withdrawing about half of the money from each of the accounts. The man wore a nice suit had a well groomed goatee; he visited ten branches over the course of two days. The woman wore a low cut blouse allowing her ample cleavage to show itself. Her skirt was short enough that the bank officers who rushed to assist her could barely decide whether to ogle her thighs or her breasts before the transactions were completed and she was gone. Several of them watched as she walked away and caught a glimpse of a butterfly tattoo on her lower back that peeked out as her well proportioned hips swayed back and forth.

The goateed man was Martin Franklin and at the end of the second day he went out for a few drinks to celebrate. He started driving home before changing his mind and deciding to stop by an old friends place instead. His wife would already be in bed asleep, so having a couple of beers with an old buddy wouldn't hurt.

He knocked on the door and was greeted warmly. After a beer and a line of cocaine he was feeling pretty good. He had just leaned back and closed his eyes when the door exploded inward and several cops came rushing in. He quickly found himself cuffed and hauled downtown. Now he sat in a small room waiting to be questioned.

The door opened and detective James Nelson walked in holding a clipboard and looking through the papers on it.

"Ouch Franklin....time for theft, B and E and armed robbery....now drug possession with intent to sell, resisting arrest, carrying a concealed weapon....my, my, my."

"Ain't you a little young to be a detective? What, your daddy the chief of police?"

The twenty-four year old detective patiently waited for Franklin to speak.

"The drugs weren't mine so there's no possession, no resisting and that was just a little pocket knife....you got nothing."

"Right, three strikes and you're out my friend. You are gonna do time for this. Don't doubt that."

Franklin sat and shook his head, thinking about his wife Karen and the kids and not seeing them again for another long stretch.

The detective was just about to speak when his partner tapped on the door and waved for him to come outside. In two minutes he came back into the interrogation room along with his partner, veteran Ben Anderson. Anderson smiled at Franklin.

"That's a nice looking goatee you have there. Very distinguished looking, it sure makes you look good on camera."

He then slid a photo across the table. Franklin looked down at the bank surveillance camera picture from one of the banks he had visited over the last two days. The color drained from his face and beads of sweat popped out on his forehead. He spoke with very little conviction.

"I don't know nothing about that."

Detective Nelson spoke softly.

"I do have a little question for you....how does twenty-five years sound? I mean, with your record....wow....well, I guess it doesn't matter much now anyways, because this is federal and the feds, oh yeah, they play for keeps."

The detective continued flipping through the papers, then closed the top folder and turned to leave.

"What about a deal?"

The detective stopped at the door.

"Deal? What do you have to deal with? You just said you don't..."

"I can't go back inside."

The detective said nothing and left the room. Ten minutes later he returned and sat down without saying anything. Franklin squirmed in his seat.

"So what have you got for us?"

"What kind of deal?"

"You know the score….that'll depend on what you have. Now I got things to do, so it's time to put up or shut up."

"Okay, so some guy comes up to me and asks if I wanna make some easy money, says all I gotta do is stroll into the bank branches and withdraw money from some accounts. I mean I gotta wife and kid to support and I needed the dough."

The detective slapped his hand on the table.

"Names?"

He slid another photo across the table.

"Who's this?"

Franklin picked up the photo of an attractive woman and scrunched up his face.

"Never seen her before in my life."

The detective stood up.

"Enjoy your time back in the joint."

"I'm telling you the truth, I don't know the woman. The guy had all the details written out, all I did was follow the instructions."

"So where is the money?"

"I met up with him after every other branch and gave him all the dough."

"We are through playing around Franklin. At your age you'll be lucky to live long enough to ever see your kid again."

"Frankie Tarasco, he's the guy. He don't even have to know it was me that gave him up. Right?"

"Where can we find this Tarasco?"

The following day Frankie Tarasco was placed under arrest. The woman that had been his second known accomplice was never apprehended and none of the stolen three hundred and ninety thousand dollars was ever recovered.

The banks were not too happy at the prospect of the public learning how easily they had been duped and pushed the prosecutor to cut a deal that would prevent an embarrassing trial. Frankie took the deal and the lighter sentence that came with it.

January 20, 1993

Martin Franklin sat at the bar of his favorite watering hole and ordered one more last round while he decided whether he had enough antifreeze inside of him to deal with the freezing cold temperature outside.

It was almost two in the morning before he pushed back from the bar and staggered out into the cold. He pulled his coat collar up as high around his head and neck as it would go. Several inches of thick wet snow covered his car. He had to yank hard in order to get the car door open as the bottom layers of snow were frozen solid.

Martin started the car and reached behind the seat for his ice scraper. He stepped back outside and began scraping the snow and ice off of the windshield never noticing the snow plow pulling away from the curb and heading his way.

Martin Franklin turned just in time to see the blade of the snow plow at waist height heading straight at him.

The blade caught him across his stomach and pinned his left arm between the edge of the blade and his car. He lost consciousness and thus never felt being nearly chopped in two.

The pick-up truck disappeared down the street as the driver pulled the woolen ski-cap off and shook out her long blonde hair. She briefly turned in the seat to look behind and her coat rode up her back exposing a brightly colored butterfly tattoo.

1997

Angelo Martin went into work on Saturday as usual in an effort to get ahead for the following week. As he walked to his office he was met by one of the young corporate officers, who accompanied him to his office.

"Mr. Martin, on behalf of Firebrand Electrics, I want to thank you for your service to the company. As you are well aware of....with the loss of many of the defense department contracts....well....cutbacks must be made and your position is being eliminated."

The young man picked through one of the many folders in his hands.

"You have four weeks of unused vacation at this time and you will receive one day of vacation for each year of service."

"You've gotta be kidding me?"

"So the total time will be seven weeks plus two days pro-rated pay."

As they spoke a security guard stepped into the office.

"Please remove your personal items. You will have fifteen minutes to vacate the premises."

"Fifteen whole minutes! How generous, after fifteen years I get fifteen minutes."

When he pulled into the driveway, the boys were

shooting baskets into the hoop mounted on the garage. He stopped the car, got out and began walking toward the house before dropping down to one knee. The boys raced to his side.

"Dad....Dad, are you okay?"

With tears in his eyes he rose to his feet and the boys helped him inside. He sat down at the kitchen table as his son Mario went to get his mom.

When Tommy came over with his wife Marion and son Ronnie, they found their neighbors in the living room.

"Angelo, what's wrong? Do we need to get you to the hospital?"

Angelo recovered enough to tell them what had happened at work.

Tommy jumped to his feet.

"I'm gonna call Pete and find out what's going on?"

"Stop it....let it go, it's over and done with."

On Monday morning another one hundred employees were sent packing in the same unceremonious fashion. Many left in silent shock, some with tears in their eyes and at least a couple of punches were thrown.

Tuesday through Thursday brought more of the same. Before it was all said and done, just over four hundred of the twelve hundred employees at this branch of the company were gone. The rest walked around like zombies, their morale was devastated.

An e-mail was sent out on Thursday afternoon, thanking everyone for their patience as the company worked through these tough times. It tried to reassure everyone that these cuts were necessary for the survival of the company.

Tommy Smith did not have the opportunity to read the e-mail. He had been let go on Wednesday.

1998

Mansfield, Ohio

Mansfield Reformatory

"614308, front and center."

Frankie Tarasco heard his number being called and ignored it.

"614308, Tarasco, get your ass up here."

Frankie stood up and moved slowly up to the guard with the proper look of non-interest pasted on his face.

"Follow me."

The guard turned and walked off. Frankie followed without question or comment. They stopped outside the wardens' office where Frankie was frisked once again. He was then told to sit.

After a few minutes the door opened and he was brought into the wardens' office. The warden sat reviewing material in a folder without looking up. He finally raised his head.

"Please have a seat, Mr. Tarasco."

The warden came out from behind his desk and walked over to the guard.

"We'll be okay; you can wait outside, thank you."

He sat down in the chair next to Frank.

"As the new warden here, I try to familiarize myself with the inmates and quite frankly I'm intrigued Mr. Tarasco. No priors until this bank computer deal. Looks like you wouldn't have been caught there if not for one of your own rolling over on you."

Frank sat in silence with little expression showing on his face.

"So many of the men incarcerated here have few if any skills that can help them to re-enter society. You.....on the other hand, have skills and I think that you are a good bet to make it back to being a productive member of the community."

"I'm curious about your skills. You see I've been leading a team right here at Mansfield in revamping the states antiquated database for prisoners. The state has thirty-two facilities and approximately fifty thousand inmates. You know we have over twenty-five hundred here alone. Anyway....it's not often that we get the opportunity to....let's say....access someone with your talents. If you're willing to lend us a hand, it will certainly go a long way toward helping you earn an early release."

That conversation led to Frank joining the wardens' team and that in turn led to him helping them over the next four months to redesign and update the entire states' prisoner database. Frank was able to set up programs that would allow for instant data and graphical analysis of the inmate population.

The warden and his team were thrilled with Franks' work. The warden became the darling of the Ohio Department of Corrections and Frankie was granted shock parole. It was the proverbial win-win situation and everyone walked away happy.

1999

Akron, Ohio

Firestone Park

The boys Mario and Ronnie were now juniors and played all the high school sports although they were not stars. They were just solid players and as such, neither one would qualify for any athletic scholarships as their high school careers came to a close.

Frankie pulled up to the Martin home and knocked on the door. Mario answered.

"Hey Mr. T, good to see you."

Frankie wrapped the young man in a big bear hug.

"How you doing kiddo? Ready for college yet, all those cute girls?"

"Nah, looking for work. You know moneys kinda tight now."

"How's your mom?"

"She's hanging in there; the chemo's wearing her down some. She sleeps a lot now."

"Where's your dad?"

"Out in the garage would be my guess."

Frankie entered the garage to find Angelo Martin sitting and staring aimlessly at the floor. He held an unopened can of beer in his hands.

"Angelo, long time no see."

"Frankie, it's been a couple of years heh?"

"Yeah well....what's happening with you? Mario

says he's not going to college. What's up with that?"

"Moneys tight, without the insurance I can't really give Maria the care she needs. I already got more bills than I can ever pay. We might have to sell the house. Mario knows the score. He's a good boy. He'll be alright."

"Can I go in and see Maria?"

"Sure, she'll be happy to see ya."

After his visit with Maria, Frankie slipped a handful of bills into Angelo's hand. He motioned for Mario to follow him as he headed out to his car.

"Here, put this in your pocket. Go out and have a good time kid. You know, if you're interested....I may be able to help you with a decent job."

"Thanks Frankie, I appreciate it. I'll let you know."

2000

Akron, Ohio

Firestone Park

Mario and Ronnie were shooting hoops in the driveway when Frankie pulled in. They came up to the car and got a big hug from their adopted uncle.

"You two are making me feel old. Getting so damn big. So what's the plan? College or working for a living?"

The boys looked at each other in silence.

"C'mon, what's up?"

"Well....we joined the army."

Frankie shook his head.

"So when did this bright idea come up?"

"Recruiters came to the school and well....with the job market and stuff, well....college just wasn't going to happen, so...."

"We'll be able to go to college after the army and they'll pay for it."

Frankie put an arm around each of the boys' shoulders and walked with them up the drive. He made them promise to keep in touch with him while they were away. He reached into his pocket and peeled off several large bills for each of them.

"You better have a good time now, before those drill instructors get a hold of your skinny asses."

The boys made it through boot camp and got stationed in Germany. Everything seemed to be going pretty good until the world changed on 9-11-2001. Each of them would eventually do two tours in Iraq and one in Afghanistan before they were able to get stateside assignments.

Over their time in the service they had not been able to share a lot with their families. On the other hand, they told Frankie most everything. Both boys were proud of their service but, disappointed by the Army's continual issuing of stop-loss orders. These effectively extended their enlistment indefinitely.

2010

Tobyhanna Army Depot, Pennsylvania

Ronnie and Mario were stationed here and found themselves exceedingly frustrated by the lack of control they had over their own futures. They shared their anger at the military with Frankie.

When Mario's mom passed away after her long battle with cancer and his request to move up his retirement date was denied, the boys' dissatisfaction intensified.

Frankie met with the boys at a quiet little bar not far from the base. They sat down at a booth in the corner away from the other patrons.

"Boys, you know I don't like what the military is doing to you anymore than you do. You're just going to have to take it."

"Tell us about it. We're not the only ones who are pissed off about it."

"Fuckin right there bro."

Frankie sat rubbing his hands together.

"What's up Frankie? You look like you've got something to say."

"Yeah, it's not like you to hold back."

"You boys know that I....uh, well, I haven't always been on the right side of the law. Been involved in a few things here and there."

"So what Frankie? We know how you've been to us and our families."

"Yeah, we don't give a shit about that. So go on and speak freely."

"I got a guy; fucking rich guy who owns about half the state of Montana and he collects guns, military gear, all kinds of shit. He fancies himself as a survivalist kinda guy. Now, over the years I've been able to acquire a few exotic things for the guy, so naturally he comes to me with his latest request."

Ronnie laughed.

"Hey, I can get ya an M1A1 Abrams tank cheap."

The boys clinked beer bottles and laughed. Frankie smiled but didn't join in their laughter.

"How about four SMAWs and let's say eight HEAA rockets?"

SMAW stood for Shoulder-launched Multipurpose Assault Weapon. It was a formidable weapon that was a portable rocket launcher or modern day bazooka. The HEAA rockets were high explosive anti armor rockets effective against tanks.

Frankie stared at them and continued on with a deadly serious look on his face.

"How about a little C-4 for good measure?"

Ronnie stared back across the table, his smile now gone.

"Right, the guy got his own fucking army or what?"

"No he's legit, maybe a little out there but, what he does have is cash. Two hundred and fifty grand."

"Yeah but ya can't spend it in Leavenworth."

"Got that shit right. Probably be tried for treason if ya get caught trying to steal those bad boys."

"I know boys, I know. I wouldn't have mentioned it....it's just that I thought that money would really help your families out. I can assure you that this guy is just gonna shoot these things off on his ranch. They are not going to end up with some terrorist group. You can trust me on that. You boys know my word is good."

Ronnie shook his head slowly.

"Okay Frankie. There's just no way, no way."

Frankie smiled.

"What....come on Frankie, what is it?"

"Well....let's just say that if I could get access to a secure computer on the base for say....twelve to fifteen minutes. Then we can make them disappear like magic. You know the military misplaces all kinds of things all the time."

Ronnie started to say no when Mario spoke up.

"Count me in."

December 2010

Tobyhanna Army Depot, Pennsylvania

The snowstorm was in full fury when Frankie pulled up to the gate in the cargo van. He showed all the correct credentials to the young Corporal who pointed him in the right direction.

Frankie backed the van up to the loading dock as Ronnie waved him into position. He stepped out holding a clipboard and walked inside the building. Mario took Frankie into a small office where Frankie sat down at the computer and quickly began typing.

Mario walked outside and helped Ronnie to load the four cases, each about the size of a guitar case, although rectangular in shape. Two small crates carrying the rockets and three cases of C-4 plastic explosives completed the order. They closed and locked the vans' rear doors and returned to the office.

The boys eyed each other nervously and stamped their feet in an attempt to keep warm and hide some of their anxiety. Frankie sat back and smiled.

"Relax boys, those items have never been in Tobyhanna and therefore cannot go missing since they never existed in the first place."

"You sure they can't trace this back here to us?"

"We're covered. I'll see you boys home for Christmas."

The van pulled away and was through the gate and off the base three minutes later. Frankie drove carefully through the early winter storm all the way back to Ohio. The boys just hoped everything would work out.

May 2011

The overnight delivery package was picked up by a courier at the shipping and receiving office of Intech Industries in San Jose, California. Intech was located in the heart of Silicon Valley. The package was taken straight to the airport where it was loaded into a larger container with several other packages. Two hours later the container was in the air and headed for Cincinnati, Ohio.

The courier there made stops in Cincinnati and then headed north towards Cleveland with the small package from Intech. As the van moved through Akron, the driver pulled off the highway and headed into a quiet residential neighborhood. The driver pulled into a tree lined drive and then backed up to the garage as the door opened. He backed into the garage and the door closed. Frankie Tarasco stepped out of the shadows and handed an envelope to the driver who pocketed it without hesitation. The driver then handed the small package back out in exchange.

Frankie took the package over to a work bench and placed it upside down. He carefully sliced through the packing tape and pulled the contents out. He took the four circuit boards aside and one by one plugged them into a slot in the computer on the bench. He sat typing for a few moments. It took three minutes to download programs on each board. Fifteen minutes later he sealed the box back up and handed it to the driver.

An hour later the package was signed for at the receiving dock of the Federal Reserve Bank in downtown Cleveland.

Anthony Barrano clocked in at four o'clock on Friday afternoon. His first stop was to check the day's maintenance work orders and then pick up his tools. He would work on those items in the banks offices until after closing at six, then head to the lobby and the public areas.

He picked up the package shipped overnight from California, carried it up to the sixth floor and entered the server room. He sat and waited until one minute after twelve before shutting down the server. After removing four screws and two clips he pulled four circuit boards out and replaced them one at a time with the new boards. At ten after twelve, the server was back on and Anthony was heading back down to clock out and head for home.

May 2011

Akron, Ohio

Downtown

Frankie sat hunched over on a small stool in the cramped back room of a dingy looking pawn shop. His eyes looked through a large lighted magnifying glass as he soldered delicate electronics on an old used computer that someone had long ago brought in for repair and then abandoned after finding it cheaper to buy a new one than to pay for repairs. He straightened up and stretched his shoulders back while rolling his head slowly from side to side. Satisfied with his efforts he stood up and walked out of the shop's rear entrance.

Later that afternoon he would meet with an aging real estate agent. Like many in the business of buying and selling real estate, the man had fallen on hard times. He perked up when the stranger told him about his company planning on relocating many workers to the area and that he would need to rent numerous properties.

Frankie spent the next two days driving the city checking out many rental properties before settling on fifteen separate residences. One thing they all had in common was at a minimum, a two car enclosed garage. Most were blocked from their neighbors prying eyes by open spaces, high fences or large hedges and trees.

Frankie wrote out rent checks each month that totaled just a bit fewer than twelve thousand dollars.

Over the next month Frankie readied them all for some temporary occupancy.

Monday June 6, 2011

Frankie sat down next to the young girl with orange spiked hair and smiled without speaking. He pulled a laptop out of the leather satchel that he carried and placed it next to the bright pink one that she was typing on.

"Morning Emily."

Emily was nineteen years old although she could pass for fourteen when she wanted or needed to. Two years earlier she had been living in California when she had been arrested for cyber crimes. Since she was still a juvenile, she had only received probation and a stern lecture from a judge who looked like a little old grandmother. Frankie had with little fanfare given her a key ring that contained keys to a car and an apartment. He told her to go about her life and that one day soon he would get in touch. That day had come one week ago.

"Morning Mr. A," she said with a hint of sarcasm as she smiled and took a sip of coffee.

He nudged his computer over toward her.

"See what you can make of this?"

She spent the next ten minutes studying the monitor, scrolling through the screens and on occasion typing furiously before commenting.

"This is some serious sh, uh, stuff here. Federal Reserve Bank systems take their security to heart. You sure they aren't on you right now?"

He ignored the question and just pointed at the screen.

"What are we following right here? Do you understand it?"

"Complex algorithms for sure," and after another minute she added, "Monitoring the shredding of old bills."

"Good. Now can you tell me how many or the amounts?"

Emily spent the next few minutes scrolling through a variety of screens chocked full of information before speaking.

"How many bills they're shredding? Wow, between twelve and eighteen million dollars worth each day. That's Monday through Friday going back for the last three weeks."

"So can you change the count?"

"Yes but….I'm not seeing the bigger picture."

"You don't need to see the big picture. Believe me it's in your best interest not to."

Emily shrugged her shoulders and hit the enter key.

"Okay, it's done."

With a single keystroke they had changed the count on the number of packets of used bills to be shredded inside the non-descript building that housed the Federal Reserve Bank where old tattered, torn, stained or otherwise damaged bills were sent to be shredded.

The bills would continue to be shredded as usual. The only difference was that instead of shredding twelve million dollars, it would actually only shred eleven million, nine hundred and ninety-nine thousand and nine hundred and ninety dollars over the course of the day.

They planned to meet up again in three days and try to determine if their changes had been detected.

Tuesday June 7, 2011

Downtown Akron

Team Nitro

Frankie Tarasco sat down at the large round wooden table and sipped on a bottle of water. Hundreds of people were walking through the downtown concert area on their lunchtime as a steel drum band played in the background. Several food vendors had scores of people waiting in line for some lunch.

The first person to join the table was a six foot seven inch giant of a man and Frankie thought that it was a good thing the table was bolted to the ground as he sat down. His name was Stanislaw Kovanic and he was the son of a Polish immigrant who fled to America during the height of the cold war. He said nothing as he looked around cautiously.

The next to take a seat was only slightly less imposing in stature. He gave up a few inches and probably fifty or so pounds to the first man but looked like he would not go easily in any fight. His name was Mark Portis and he sat down with a mumbled grunt as his hello. The two big men eyed each other warily until the next member of their team joined them.

He was several inches shorter than either of the other two but held his own in the weight department. His massive girth held upwards of three hundred pounds and had long ago earned him the nickname of

Tiny. Huffing and puffing, he sat down and placed his meaty arms on the tabletop while he tried to catch his breath.

Thomas Pierce was the last man to join them. He was also tall at six foot four inches and although muscular he was not as solid looking as the others. His hair was cut short and upon a long pointed nose sat reflective sunglasses that shielded his eyes. He also took a seat without comment.

Frankie got right to business, he pointed at the red faced Tiny, "You will refer to me as Mr. A from now on, you are number One and team leader. You will handle the detonations and all the electronics. We've already gone over the equipment needed and have everything ready to go."

He nodded at Kovanic, the tallest member of the group, "You'll be number Two and between you and Three," here he indicated Portis, "and Four", this time nodding at the last man to sit, "and me, we will set the charges in all the locations."

Frankie rolled out a map of the city that had a series of bright red dots scattered across it and he began passing out the assignments to each man. Two, Three and Four would be doing the majority of the field work with One coordinating everything. They spent the next hour talking through the details before Mr. A was satisfied enough to call an end to the meeting.

Thursday June 9, 2011

Frankie entered the small coffee shop and went to sit down in the booth next to Emily. She looked up and smiled.

He barely had a chance to take a breath when she volunteered, "They have no idea anything's up. So I think we're ready for phase two, how about you?"

He replied without hesitation, "Do it."

Frankie rose up and left without another word as Emily again sent a new command through the air that would once more disrupt the count as damaged bills fluttered through the shredders. This time the difference would be slightly more than the ten dollars from their previous command. Within one weeks time it would think it was shredding fifteen million dollars when in actuality it was only destroying ten million.

Friday June 10, 2011
Downtown Akron

The National Bank building in downtown Akron stands twenty-seven stories to a total of three hundred and thirty feet, the television and cell tower atop it bring it to a height of four hundred forty-two feet. At ten in the morning an apparent malfunction in the heating and air conditioning system caused the temperature to drop by ten degrees. A few minutes later the temperature had returned to normal. This was followed by a rise of twenty degrees. These swings continued until eleven fifteen when the entire system shut itself down.

A man with a bushy walrus mustache and graying hair hanging out from under his ball cap stepped up to the security guard and setting down his tool bags and computer satchel, handed over his AAA Heating and Air Conditioning identification card. The guard wiped sweat from his forehead and looked at the card that said the man was Patrick Dent and then back at the man wearing a white jumpsuit with a AAA logo and the name Pat stitched upon it.

"You gonna get this thing fixed?"

"That's the plan."

Patrick Dent pulled the pens and small screwdrivers from his front pocket and placed them into the small plastic tub along with a large ring of keys, his cell phone and an assortment of change from his pocket. He walked through the metal detector and picked up his things as the guard behind the scanner looked at the x-ray of his tool bags with a cursory examination.

Ten minutes later he sat in the sub-basement room that housed much of the buildings electronic controls. He pulled out his laptop computer and plugged it into a special outlet. While the computer booted up he chatted aimlessly with Jimmy, the maintenance technician who was assigned to assist him.

Jimmy watched over Patrick's shoulder as he scrolled through various blueprints and diagrams of the buildings piping and electrical equipment and tried to understand what he was looking at as Patrick would occasionally nod his head or mumble an uh-huh or okay. Patrick pushed his chair back from the counter.

"First you need to take me to the roof where the main unit is and then you will need to come back down here and keep an eye on this screen."

Here he pointed at the laptop.

"I'll let you know when; you'll need to let me know which of the circuits is firing when. Simple as that. Alright?"

Jimmy rubbed the back of his neck while a look of bewilderment played across his face.

"Okey dokey."

Jimmy led Patrick up to the roof unlocking two padlocked doors to gain access to the unit on the roof.

"Okay thanks, you go back down. It'll take me a few minutes to get set up anyway and then I'll give you a holler."

Jimmy gave a thumb up signal and left the roof. Patrick waited thirty seconds before walking across the roof to yet another locked gate surrounding the cell phone and television tower. It took him about ten seconds to pick the lock and get inside.

He placed a small satchel into a hidden crevice and ran two wires from it out to a small piece of conduit piping with a cap on it. Unscrewing the cap, he pulled two wires and connected both sets together.

He flipped open his phone and dialed the number Jimmy had given him as he locked the gate behind him.

"Okay Jimmy, are you ready? Just let me know what you see on the screen."

"Gotcha boss."

Patrick pulled a small device from one of the tool bags. It looked like an amperage meter that most technicians carried to test electrical circuits. He pressed one of its buttons. Jimmy immediately responded.

"The P one circuit just lit up."

"Okay Jimmy, going for two now."

Another button push brought another reply.

"Two just lit up."

"Great Jimmy, I think that's about it. You can come back up and get me."

He put his tools back into his bags and walked to the main roof access door to wait for his escort. Jimmy was back in only a few minutes and after locking up they headed back down to the control room. Patrick spent a few minutes appearing to scroll through the schematic diagrams until Jimmy lost interest.

Within fifteen minutes the temperature in the building had stabilized and Patrick was on his way out the door while receiving a hearty thank you from the security detail on duty. No one seemed to notice that he had one less bag with him on his exit.

Several blocks away Patrick pulled the wig and mustache off and tossed them onto the seat along with the identification card containing a picture of a person that he no longer resembled.

Friday   June 17, 2011
K Mart Supercenter, Rt. 91 Akron

A white van turned into the K-Mart parking lot and circled slowly before pulling into a parking space that was ten spots away from any other vehicles. Like people do when they have a new car and don't want anybody to accidentally open their door and scratch their new baby. Only, this van wasn't new. In fact it was an older model with more than a few dents and dings already. There were no signs or bumper stickers on it, nothing to distinguish it from any other van. The windows were tinted slightly and it was a bit difficult to clearly see the driver inside.

Willie Anderson was in the same spot now for the third straight day and the twelfth in the last three weeks. Yesterday he had driven a Ford Taurus, the day before it was a Dodge minivan. The time was four-fifty in the late afternoon, early evening. He pulled out a clipboard and his binoculars and checked his watch. He noted the time and then watched as Sally, Karen and Cathy began their routine.

Sally was the store's daytime manager. She was a five foot two dynamo, always smiling and called everyone Hun. Customers and employees alike, everybody was Hun. "Can I help you hun, what do you need hun, thank you hun, hun, hun." She was always in motion and knew her job inside and out. Karen was the floor manager and worked across shifts. She was just as efficient as Sally although she didn't move quite as fast. She was a big woman and she was also everyone's buddy. Cathy was the assistant store manager and with a degree in accounting did the majority of the bookwork and counting of the cash drawers. She rarely smiled and kept the chit chat to a minimum. She was prim and proper and all business. When others tried to make small talk with her, she would generally tilt her head down and raise her eyes to look at them over the top of the half glasses perched on her nose. Without saying a word, she would then return to her task. That usually put an end to any attempts at conversation.

There was a store security guard on duty. He was about six-five and weighed somewhere in the neighborhood of two-fifty. Willie had decided that his name should be Studley although his badge identified him as Officer Grimes. He mostly just wandered around aimlessly but, stood next to the door to the office during the register exchanges. He kept a very close eye on the young female cashiers. Occasionally during slow periods he would spend some time with one of the female stockers in one of the back storage areas.

At five on the dot Sally would come from the office area just inside of the front doors followed by the next shift's cashier. They would head to register number one. She would ring out the register and the cashier would take his or her cash drawer and the register tapes and wait until Sally had got the next cashier set up and ready to go. Then they would walk back to the office area where either Sally would use her key to open the door or Cathy would buzz them in. Sally would then take the next cashier out and go down the line. There were twelve cash registers in place. On most days they only had four to six operating. With the summer season in full swing, they had picked up to between seven and ten registers open. Today they had some big pre-fourth of July sales going on and there were nine cashiers in operation. It took anywhere from two to four minutes for her to close out each register and get the next shift going.

As Sally was handling the front registers, Karen would walk out to the various other departments. She started in the jewelry department with the same routine. Closing out the register and then walking that employee back to the front office. Then it was off to the electronics department, lay-a-way and the seasonal area. After all these departments were closed out, the only two remaining registers were at the customer service area right in front of the office. Whoever finished with their registers first would close out these two.

Willie jotted down the times of each cashier entering the office area. Today there were a total of fifteen separate cash drawers being counted out. By six o'clock they were complete and all of the money was inside standard bags for their pick up by armored car. Like clockwork, the armored car pulled up at no sooner than six-oh-two and no later than six-oh-seven. The passenger door opened and a short skinny guy got out. Willie referred to him as Barney. Barney went to the rear door and opened it and out climbed another security guard. He appeared to be somewhere between sixty-five and ninety and Willie called him Gramps. Barney and Gramps would walk inside and be greeted by Sally with, "How are ya hun?" Studley would nod and walk with them until they were back outside the door with the day's deposits. He would then offer to walk the ladies going off duty, to their cars. Barney and Gramps would open the rear doors and Gramps would climb in and the doors would close behind him. They would be on the move within five minutes of their arrival.

The stop at K-Mart was the armored cars next to last stop of its run before heading to its company's main vault downtown. As the armored car drove off, a white pickup truck passed by Willie and the driver gave a wave. Willie started up the van, pulled out behind the truck and the two vehicles drove off.

Willie only knew the driver by as number One and number One only knew him as Three. They followed a seemingly random path before pulling into the driveway of a house and the backing into the last two bays of a three car garage. The drivers went inside the house and went over the days observations with the man they only knew as Mr. A.

West Akron Mall

Friday June 24, 2011

Jack Wesley was a forty-four year old man sitting in the food court of the West Akron mall. He sipped on a soft drink as he waited for his wife and two teenage daughters to complete their shopping orgy. He had joined the Akron police department at the age of twenty and he now sat daydreaming about retirement in just six short years. The girls would be off to college by then and he hoped to be semi-retired while enjoying the good life in some warm, tropical climate.

He shook the cup, rattling the ice around as he noisily sipped the last of the soda. His eyes shifted to a set of glass double doors with stenciled lettering simply stating, "Mall Offices". The doors were located at the end of the food court and just before the first of many stores in the huge multilevel mall.

Three burly uniformed armed guards came out through the doors. One guard walked out and held the door open as the second man strode confidently out, his right hand resting on his holstered weapon and his eyes scanning their surroundings. The next guard walked out with a dolly that had three large metal boxes stacked and strapped to it. He followed two steps behind while the guard who had held the door fell in at the rear of the column.

Jack quickly turned his attention from the three security guards and focused on the crowd. His eyes found themselves drawn to a young woman with green and purple streaks in her hair who sat at a table holding her phone up in front of her. From his angle he could see that she appeared to be videotaping them as they walked by. She stood up as they passed by and began walking behind them.

Jack Wesley casually stood up and headed for the doors. He watched as the woman stopped just outside of the second of two sets of doors and waited until the last of the guards had disappeared inside of their armored truck. As the truck pulled away, the woman walked to the curb and got into the front seat of a late model sedan. Jack could only make out half of the license plate number. The other half was conveniently covered in mud.

Jack stood watching as the armored truck pulled out onto the main road, the sedan following two cars back. Rubbing his chin, Jack returned to his seat to continue waiting for the women in his life.

Friday June 24, 2011

Frankie Tarasco rubbed his hand over his mouth and turned off the television and the local evening news. He knew that he had made a mistake that needed rectified. He had thought through almost any scenario that might occur and had made many contingency plans along the way. He grabbed his jacket and headed out to the car.

As he drove he thought back upon his decision to bring Mark Portis in on this job. Portis had been trained in the Army but had been busted out with a dishonorable discharge for getting drunk and punching out a senior officer. Portis freely admitted that he would have punched him out even if he had been sober.

He was a six foot three hulk of a man with a face that looked to have been hit by a shovel. A flattened boxer's nose and a nasty scar on his right cheek all added to his imposing presence. He was an expert with explosives and demolition and as one might expect, preferred to work alone.

Frankie pulled into the driveway of the small house in the Goodyear Heights area of the city, parked the car and went inside to find Portis sitting at the kitchen table drinking a beer.

"Hey Mark, how ya doing?"

"Alright Mr. A."

"So how'd it go yesterday?"

"We're all set."

"Yeah! I heard some chatter."

"Nah, we're good Mr. A. That nosy bitch shoulda minded her own business. Shouldn't a been on that roof anyway."

"So tell me exactly what happened."

"I'm on the roof, just finished setting the explosives and the remote detonator and I look up and there she is. She's looking at me with a puzzled expression. She asks me what exactly am I doing. I stood up, you know I was down on my knees. So I stand up and she starts backing away."

"I took one step towards her and she says she's calling the cops. She made it two or three steps when I grabbed her, just clamped my hand over her mouth and she went to sleep, real peaceful like. I didn't want to leave her there in case the cops would get too nosey and start poking around. So I carry my stuff to the stairs, first I tried holding her around the waist with one hand and dragging her down but, that was too slow. So I just tossed her over my shoulder, dropped her behind some bushes. Nobody seen nothing Mr. A. All the charges are set just like we planned it."

Frankie nodded, "Good, good. You did what you had to do. You just hang here and stay outta sight for a few days and we'll be good."

Frankie walked over and opened up the refrigerator door. When the door closed, he stood holding a pistol with a silencer. Mark Portis never had a chance to react before the first of two slugs tore through his chest.

Monday June 27, 2011
Team Gold

Mr. A picked up a soda at the counter of the fast food restaurant and went outside to sit at one of the large round metal tables. Within five minutes four oversized men joined him, the first three took a seat without comment. The last man had a large round face with a big smile pasted on it.

"Morning fellers, what no happy meals?"

The men allowed their concentration to waver as the loud throaty rumble of a Harley Davidson pulled up near their table. The woman rider wore full leathers even in the June heat. They watched as she pulled off her helmet and shook out her long dark hair. She pulled off her jacket and tossed it across the bikes seat. The tight tank top she wore caused a few smiles among the men as she walked over to them.

The stern faced Mr. A just stated, "Take a seat please."

He pointed to a man that was just forty years old, although most would have guessed him to be in his late fifties due to the deeply etched crow's feet and his leathery skin that he had earned though some seventy bouts inside the ring. While he had the looks of just another washed up, punch-drunk fighter, his mind was still sharp and when he handed out orders they were rarely questioned.

"You will be number One and team leader, and you will be number Two and driver."

This last was directed at an olive skinned man with wavy black hair slicked back, he also had a pencil thin mustache. Mr. A turned to the youngest man in the group, whose blonde hair cascaded down around his shoulders, "Number Three will handle the entry with Four's assistance. Number Four stood six foot five and his clothing bulged in all directions as he sat listening.

For the next thirty minutes Mr. A gave out step by step instructions that covered every detail. The team then spent a few minutes asking questions that he answered easily until everyone was satisfied. They planned to meet again the following day.

Tuesday June 28, 2011
Team Mall

Mr. A walked casually through the mall like every other shopper until he came to the ice skating rink. He took a seat and watched as several people attempted to skate around the rink. He was soon joined by a well dressed man named Sam Taylor; they were in turn joined by a tall bald headed man and the two sat across from Mr. A.

Taylor smiled broadly, "Damn Mr. A, sitting here with two brothers, you stick out like a sore thumb." The two men laughed as Frankie shook his head.

A tall man with a wild tangled head of hair and a two day growth of beard plopped down in the seat between the two black men.

"Looks like you got an Oreo sandwich here."

Frankie ignored the comment and placed one of the mall's own brochures onto the table and began reviewing the plan with the team. Sam Taylor would be the team leader and driver of the van that would serve as the getaway vehicle. The man in the middle would be driving the blocking vehicle and would be known as number Three and the last man would be Two and he would handle the main assault on the armored car. Forty minutes later all were nodding in assent and ready to go.

Tuesday June 28, 2011
Team Gold

Frankie pulled into the large packed parking lot and parked on the periphery from where he could observe a wide portion of the vehicles. He waited twenty minutes before heading inside the building. The sounds of music blaring mixed with a cacophony of bowling balls crashing into the pins in the cavernous sixty-four lane bowling alley.

He walked past billiard tables and video games until he came to a pair of lanes where six people sat without bowling. Frankie sat down on one of the plastic chairs and leaned forward as the six would be bowlers leaned in to hear over the sounds bombarding them.

This was the second meeting for this group so no introductions were necessary. Frankie leaned back in his chair and then slowly leaned sideways so as to look under the table. Everyone else followed suit and Frankie shook his head now looking across at team member number Four. He was an intimidating six foot six and weighed in somewhere north of three hundred pounds.

"How in the hell is that chair holding you up?"

"Ah, Mr. A, I'm lighter that I look."

This brought a chorus of laughter as Frankie/Mr. A pulled his chair back up to the table and taking a more serious tone he spoke to the group, "Alright One, what's our status?"

One filled him in on the teams' surveillance of the last few nights and a couple of others added comments as well. Number Five, the only woman on the team spoke up, "Also did some checking into the history of the Gold Partners. Seems they originally were going to name their store, The G-Spot but, then they figured that men would never be able to find it."

Mr. A rolled his eyes while number One scowled and said, "Let's stick to business."

Less than thirty minutes later Frankie had given them their last instructions and let them know that Friday would be the day.

Wednesday June 29, 2011

11:30 AM

Goodyear Heights Metropolitan Park

Team Fed

Frankie parked his car and walked out into the park carrying a medium size red and white cooler and a roll of paper under his arm. He smiled as he thought he must look like an architect stopping by the park for a bit of lunch. He took a seat at one of the picnic tables that sat under a lovely shade tree. He watched as a large group of high school cross country runners raced past.

Sitting the rolled papers aside he opened the cooler and retrieved a bottle of water. He sat back and sipped the cool water slowly as four men and one woman made their way over to his table from various areas of the parking lot. He waved each one to take a seat at the large wooden table and they did so.

"Thank you, you each know me as Mr. A and I personally selected each of you for this job."

Frankie pointed at the man to his right who easily stood six foot five and weighed in at about two hundred and thirty pounds of solid muscle. His hair was now pulled tightly back in a long ponytail that hung well down his back.

"This is your team leader, you will refer to him as One."

The three remaining men and the small dark haired woman eyed each other cautiously although the shortest of the men had a sarcastic smirk on his face as he spoke up.

"I just gotta tell ya that I never worked no job before where I didn't know nobody. Makes me uneasy ya know."

Mr. A smiled.

"I think that's understood number Two and a sentiment probably shared by the others as well. I chose each of you as individuals and as part of a team. I've already met with each one of you and have given you enough information to make sure that you were interested. If you're ready I will fill you in on all the details?"

He paused for a moment and when no one dissented, he unrolled his blueprints. Placing a finger on the map he started in on a well rehearsed recitation.

"You're all familiar with the area. The route starts at the Federal Reserve in Cleveland at four-thirty. One hour transit time to stop one here," he tapped a small circled number one on the map before continuing, "Three more stops prior to arrival at our destination at between one and four minutes after six."

This time a rugged looking man with a brown bushy beard shook his head and Frankie paused.

"Something you want to say three?"

"Sorry to burst your bubble but you're fucked. I don't know where you got your information about the route but, well it's somebody's fucking fantasy."

He stopped talking and smiled widely showing off several gaps where teeth were missing.

"Those guards don't know their routes two days ahead of time, or one day ahead or one hour ahead. They don't get their route until they are ready to roll."

The last of the men also looked to be no stranger to lifting heavy weights as a way to pass the time spoke up.

"What makes you such an expert?"

"About four or five years ago there was a big armored car heist where several of the guards were found guilty, anyway one of em ended up in the cell next to me. Told me all about that shit. They don't even get the route over the radio. They got these computers that generate random routes so nobody, I mean nobody knows. The route pops up on their GPS and off they go. So whoever told you they knew the route was full of shit."

Frankie leaned forward.

"Four, thank you for that. Everything you say is absolutely true. Now let's stop wasting time here. I am telling you that it's handled. You just show up according to plan and the armored car will be there for you."

For the next seventy minutes Frankie went over all of the details of the plan. He stopped over and over to ask the crew questions to ensure that they knew what to do and when to do it. He patiently answered every question they had.

Wednesday June 29, 2011

2:00 PM

Munroe Falls Metropolitan Park

Team K-Mart

Frankie walked over to an unoccupied picnic bench and took a seat. He absentmindedly looked out over the lake at the hundreds of people splashing and playing in the water. In the next few minutes four men joined him at the table.

"Gentlemen you all know me as Mr. A. I've brought each of you in on this and I have briefed each of you with the same information."

He pointed at the shortest man in the group, a dark haired Latino fellow who flashed a smile featuring two gold teeth.

"Number One will be the team leader."

Number One was actually Luis Reyes. He was a former high school phenom at the quarterback position whose coach had said he was the best leader he had ever seen. His teammates loved him and he was headed to a major college program when he blew out a knee. The recruiters stopped coming around and Luis got nailed when he was hanging out with some buddies and the cops broke in. When a large cache of drugs and weapons were found he was charged along with all the others.

He was soon kicked out of school and his life spiraled out of control until he ended up in prison. While serving out his sentence his parents both became ill and his mother passed away. Word of his situation made its way to a friendly ear and he received an early parole just in time to visit with his father in the last days of his life.

Willie Anderson as number Three gave out the details of his surveillance and Frankie assigned numbers Two and Four with their duties. He rolled out a large map and began reviewing all of the details of the plan.

After only forty-five minutes of discussion and evaluation, the team headed off having reached agreement about the plan. Each member carried an envelope with concise instructions about where and when to meet the following day.

Wednesday June 29

Akron Police Station

Detective James Nelson sat at his desk typing up a report when a fellow detective sat down in the chair next to him.

"Got a minute?"

"Whattayagot?"

"Not really sure, my bullshit detector must be off today...oh well."

Detective Martin Adams held up a folder in his hand and shook it.

"A real piece of work here. His rap sheet is as long as your arm, did two years in Mansfield for armed robbery of a liquor store, gets banged again for robbing a bar full of patrons and shooting off every round in his weapon while out of his mind on meth. First degree felony gets him five to ten in the state pen Supermax in Youngstown."

Adams closed the folder shaking his head.

"So that's old news. Now narcotics has some mid level dealers under surveillance with a hidden camera and in walks our hero flashing a wad of Benjamins. So when they move in he gets nabbed with enough coke in his pocket to get him sent back to the joint again. Now he says he wants to play let's make a deal."

Nelson leaned back and stretched.

"So what's he got?"

"First up he says he don't know no names. Says some nameless stranger approaches him and well, you should just let him tell ya."

Transcript of interrogation of prisoner Lawrence "Larry" Keller (herein noted as LK) and Detective James Nelson (herein noted as DN.

DN: I'm Detective Nelson, so let's start all over again okay Mr. Keller?

LK: Sure, sure. Like I was saying, guy comes up to me outta the blue. I don't know him from Adam, never seen him before and he just stands there staring. First I was gonna get in his face ya know but, he had a look. A hard look like I seen before ya know. A guy that you don't necessarily want to fuck with if ya don't hafta. Finally I just ask, "What?" The guy just gives me a smile and says, "I'm waiting for a thank you." So I start laughing, "Why should I thank you?" He says, "Who do you think arranged your release from the joint?" I'm like, "What joint?" The guy tells me what wing, cell number and who else was in my cell, shit you don't know if you ain't been there ya know. So I smile right back, "So why me? You my fairy godmother or something?" I thought that was pretty clever ya know.

DN: What's his name?

LK: Just said to call him Mr. A. I'm like whatever. But that was later on, first he says he was kinda like them college football coaches always on the lookout for talent. So I'm like, "What special talent I got that you need?" He says, "You're a pro, cool under pressure and that's what I need." I'm like, "Need for what?" "A big job," he says. "Four man team, your cut will be fifty Gs minimum and maybe a whole lot more." Now I gotta tellya, I was smiling at the sound a that when he steps up real close. He's staring me right in the eyes, "I treat my people right but once you're in, I expect loyalty and a tight lip. Not a fucking word to anybody." I'm like, "Count me in, not a prob, ya know." So that's when he says he's Mr. A. That's about it, says he will get in touch with me within a week and that's when I'll get more details. Then he pulls out an envelope and hands it to me. Two grand up front money.

DN: What's this Mr. A look like?"

LK: Ah, oh, about....six feet or so.

DN: I'm tired of this fantasy bullshit. You're making this up as you go.

LK: No, no, I swear it's true.

DN: Then give me a fucking description now or you can rot in prison.

Larry Keller then gave the detective as complete a description as he could or at least would.

Afterward the detectives sat around discussing whether to believe any of his story and if so, what to do about it. They decided on a brief list of things to check on first.

1-look into his prison release to see if there was anything fishy about it

2-look at a listing of former prisoners who had been there at the same time as Keller, focus on those with last names starting with the letter A, then inmates with first names starting with A

3-look into Keller's background a little deeper

They planned to reconvene tomorrow and go from there.

Thursday June 30

10:00 AM

The bluish glare from the monitor cast an eerie glow upon Emily's face as she sat typing furiously in the darkened room. Her fingers flew across the keyboard as her eyes remained locked in on the screen in front of her. She paused long enough to drain the contents of a large canned energy drink in one continuous swallow.

She brushed the purple and green bangs from her face attempting to tuck them behind her ears with little success before resuming yet another attack on the keyboard.

It would be two hours before she would sit back and stretch. After lighting a cigarette she slowly reviewed her work with a sense of satisfaction and admiration.

Finally she picked up her cell phone and sent a short text that simply stated, READY.

Thursday June 30, 2011

12:00 PM

Goodyear Heights Metropolitan Park

Frankie sat at the table with the large city of Akron road map spread out upon it. Around the table stood eight men, none of them knew each other. They stood silently as Frankie, who they only knew as Mr. A, spoke.

"Gentlemen, I've already given each of you the same talk. No names, no personal information, just discuss the job and nothing else. Is that crystal clear to everyone?"

Frankie took his time looking from face to face, receiving a nod, a wave or a verbal okay from each man in turn. When he was satisfied, he tapped his index finger on the map.

"You are all familiar with the highways in town. Four of you have been chosen to drive a semi with trailer and the other four to drive vehicles."

Frankie picked up an orange marker and drew a circle around what was known as the central interchange, where two of the main highways crossed. His hand moved up toward Route 8 Southbound just north of the interchange and drew another circle. He pointed at the tallest man in the room and then across from him at the shortest man.

"Number One and Number Two. Ones drives the rig and Two drives the vehicle. Two pulls up on the right side of One right about here and signals. He then pulls ahead while One angles the rig across all lanes effectively blocking all traffic. Two backs up and One exits the rig with the keys and gets into the vehicle. You will be given a specific route to follow that will take you to a drop-off for the vehicle. I will go over that individually with the two of you. Once there you will be paid in full and the job will be over."

He paused for a moment.

"Any questions from either of you?"

Number One raised his hand like a little kid in school and Frankie waved him on.

"What about the rig?"

"I will give you the exact location of the rig along with the when and where to meet up with Two. Two will drive you to the rig. All the details of the drop-off will be explained at that time. No team will know the details of any other team. Are we clear?"

None of the men moved a muscle and Frankie continued. Moving his hand down, he drew another circle. This time he pointed at a muscular man with a huge brown beard and a Latino man with a thin mustache.

"Three drives the rig and Four the vehicle. You'll be heading North on 77. Same thing, place the rig across all lanes right here. Get into the vehicle and follow the directions to a drop site. Clear?"

Both men nodded silently and Frankie turned his attention to an older heavyset man and young man with long blond hair hanging out from under his dew rag.

"Five in the rig, Six in the vehicle. Same thing again going 76 west. Right here. Got it?"

The two men glanced at each other briefly and nodded. Frankie made another circle on the map and spoke to the remaining two men.

"Seven gets the rig and Eight the vehicle. Right here on 76 heading east. Okay?"

Two more nods came back at him and he leaned back in his chair.

"I got a few more things here. This is an easy job, if you just follow the directions and do as you're told, you'll each walk away with twenty-five hundred bucks. The rigs are clean and so are the vehicles. Worst case scenario and you get pinched, all they got is abandoning a rig on the highway. No wallets, no ID's, no cell phones, nothing on you during the job. No weapons. ARE WE CLEAR, NO FUCKING GUNS!"

Frankie stood up abruptly.

"I am not kidding around. No weapons. Are we clear?"

Once more he slowly moved his gaze from one man to the next until he was satisfied.

"Good, good. This is a cakewalk fellas. Easy money. You get this one right, I can guarantee more jobs in the future."

He reached into his inside coat pocket and pulled out eight envelopes and handed one to each man.

"Here's the agreed upon five hundred for each of ya. You'll each get the remaining two grand when you drop off the vehicles. I will contact each of you tomorrow between ten and noon and give you the final details."

Thursday June 30

Akron Police Station

The three detectives, James Nelson, his partner Beth Woodson and Martin Adams sat down together to review the Keller case. Nelson spoke up first.

"What have we got so far?"

Adams flipped open a note pad and shook his head.

"Our boy Larry Keller was convicted of first degree felony, that's mandatory prison time of three to ten, he gets five to fifteen because he's a repeat offender. Lo and behold he gets paroled after nine months. Really no way to track how, I mean his name pops up on the parole list along with about twenty-two hundred others every month. Something is definitely rotten smelling about this and it's going to take some real digging to find it. Also with that sentence he's supposed to get mandatory post release control for five years and he gets zip, nada, nothing. Just released early and no PO follow up."

Woodson followed up.

"Any ideas on how he could have slipped through the cracks like this if it wasn't done on purpose?"

"Like I said there's over twenty-six thousand inmates getting paroled every year. Over sixty percent serve one year or less. He should have never gotten out without serving his minimum sentence. Then in the Akron area there are over five thousand parolees and less than ninety PO's, you do the math and you see how he could slip through. If he doesn't show up on the computer screen then he doesn't exist."

Woodson added that she had spent the morning going through prison records with no success looking for prisoners who matched any of their criteria.

Nelson noted that although Keller was a career criminal and two time felon, he really was just your ordinary small potatoes low life, certainly not some special catch for some big time crime boss.

"We only have another hour before he will be released on bond unless we are going to cut a deal with him."

It took the three detectives about two minutes to decide that even though his prison release seemed odd, they didn't really believe his story and since he would soon be headed back behind bars, it wasn't worth pursuing any further.

Friday July 1

3:48 AM

The cell phone buzzed hard enough to rattle across the night stand before a female voice stated, "Incoming call". James Nelson opened one eye briefly before blindly stabbing his hand out from under the sheets and tapping it around until it found its intended target. Pulling the phone to his face caused the phone charger cord to be yanked away and the face of the smart phone blinded him briefly.

He blinked a couple of times before sliding his thumb across the surface. Detective Martin Adams was the caller.

"Nelson here."

"Sorry to wake you but I think we have a bit of a situation developing."

Sitting up on the edge of the bed and stifling a yawn he tried to become a little more alert.

"Okay what have you got?"

"First off I fell asleep at six last night and the wife just let me sleep on the couch. Anyways I wake up at two in the morning and I'm wide awake, so I figure why not come in and get caught up on paperwork while it's quiet. So I'm going through a stack of arrest records and I come up on ....hold on a sec ....Percival Samuel Taylor. Name ring a bell? I didn't figure it would, anyway he's a piece a work, about thirty traffic citations and tada, four DUI's, suspended license the whole nine yards. He's one of those clowns that likes to do wheelies on his bike at a hundred miles an hour, fancies himself as a daredevil. You still with me?"

"Barely, I take it you're going to come to a point at some time?"

"Yeah, so he gets nailed again for DUI. Found him sitting at a red light, passed out behind the wheel. He also has almost five thousand cash on him. So when they question him the next morning about where he came up with all the money since surprise, surprise, he doesn't have any place of employment, he tells them a story. Get ready."

Having already gone to the bathroom and splashed water on his face, he now sat on the edge of the bathtub holding his head in his hands.

"I can hardly wait."

"Well he tells them some guy comes up to him and says, hold on so I get this quote right ....you have the skills that I need. So Percy being the funny guy that he apparently is, asks the guy why he needs somebody to drink beer, cause like that country song, he's pretty good at doing that. The guy tells him that he needs a driver for a job. All he needs to do is drive the getaway car for a team after they complete their part of the job. Tells him he will guarantee him some big money and fronts him five grand. Here's the best part, says the guy only wants to be called Mr. A."

Nelson shot straight up.

"You are shitting me right?"

"Not about this amigo."

"Alright let me call Woodson and we'll be in ASAP. We need to pull this Precival guy out of his cell right now for a little chat."

"Ahh, well not so fast. I already checked. He posted bail and flew the coop yesterday."

"Well get an address for him and for Keller and we'll go pick both of them up this morning."

Friday July 1, 2011

3:58 PM

Federal Reserve Bank, Cleveland, Ohio

Truck 175FRB723CO backed up to the dock as usual and it's four man crew double checked the tag numbers as two metallic carts loaded with bags were then transferred into compartments inside the back of the armored truck. Four satchels each fourteen inches wide by fourteen inches long and twenty-two inches high and each strapped to its own dolly were also checked off and loaded. Two of the crew entered the rear and closed the door behind them while the other two stepped up into the cab. After the standard radio check-in and verification of passwords had been completed, truck number 175 rolled out of the secured facility at 4:06 PM. The secure encrypted GPS system mapped out their route and told them that they were scheduled to make drop offs at four banks in the Akron area and return empty at 7:15 PM.

None of the four men knew the amounts inside any of the bags or satchels. None knew that inside each of the four satchels was ten million dollars worth of one hundred dollar bills that according to the Federal Reserve Bank computer system no longer existed.

Friday July 1, 2011

4:00 PM

Summit Count Courthouse

Detective James Nelson sat in the witness seat held up his hand and swore the oath. He had been waiting nearly three and a half hours to give his testimony in a shooting that had taken place nearly a year ago. His had only been a minor part in the investigation and arrest but, his testimony would be vital to confirm earlier witnesses recollections. His time on the stand was less than twenty-five minutes.

He called his partner Beth Woodson as he walked out of the courthouse and received a recap of her day's fruitless effort to find either Percy Taylor or Larry Keller. He decided to call it a day and surprise his family by joining them for dinner.

Friday July 1, 2011

4:00 PM

Team Fed

The four men of Team Fed met up at their safe house per the instructions each had received two days before. They sat down in the kitchen to go over the plans once more. The tall man with the long ponytail known as number One went to the fridge and pulled out a bottle of water. He asked if anyone else wanted one before sitting back down at the kitchen table.

The man known as Three sat scratching his neck which was buried under his unruly brown beard. He cleared his throat loudly.

"Say boss-man, we got a little problem here."

Number One smiled across the table but stayed silent with his hands folded in his lap.

"See, the way I figure it ….well we're the ones putting our asses on the line. We stand to be the ones going back to the joint, so I'm not sure about splitting the take up like the big man planned. I mean we get fifty percent to split four ways. That's bullshit!"

He pointed across the table at One.

"So get his ass on the phone and tell him the arrangement is gonna change."

One raised his right hand up and it now held a forty-five automatic which he pointed at Three. Three started to say something but, the words never left his lips as the bullet tore through his heart and his chair tipped over backward. He was dead before his head smacked into the floor with a resounding thud.

One calmly sat the weapon down on the table and smiled at Two and Four who both had jumped up and scrambled back from the table.

"Anybody else have a problem with the arrangements?"

Two offered two thumbs up in return and Four grinned easily as he replied, "Nah I'm cool with that."

One pulled his cell phone out and dialed a preprogrammed number. He proceeded to relay what had just happened to Mr. A. He nodded his head several times and mumbled a couple of uh-huhs before the conversation was ended.

"Looks like we're getting us a new partner fellas. Mr. A says that we should proceed to the site as planned."

Friday July 1, 2011
4:45 PM
Team K-Mart

Team leader Luis Reyes opened the door as the last of his four man team entered the house and they wasted no time before they once more began reviewing the plan in detail. About ten minutes later, Two slipped off of his chair and dropped to the floor on his hands and knees. In seconds his forehead was pressed to the cool linoleum and his right fist tapped the floor while his left hand was pressed to his side.

"What the hell's the matter man?"

Three knelt down beside him and looked up at the team leader.

"Well One, what now?"

"Let's get him up onto the couch first."

Two raised his head up and took several slow deep breathes blowing each one out steadily. After a few seconds he spoke up weakly.

"Kidney stones, had'em twice before. I need to go to the hospital."

Reyes slowly shook his head side to side as the other men helped him up. Two pointed to the bathroom and they half carried him to the doorway where he managed to go inside and closed the door.

"Now what do we do?"

The men were still shaking their heads when a thumping sound came from the bathroom and they raced back and One put his shoulder to the door and banged it open.

Two lay face down on the floor with his pants down around his ankles. He then pulled himself up in to the fetal position while moaning. As he lay on his side his face was ghostly white and beads of perspiration gleamed on his forehead. Once more he croaked out the words.

"Need to go to the hospital."

One walked back down the hallway past the other two men and pulled out a cell phone. One minute later he rejoined the rest of his team in the crowded bathroom. Two now lay on his back with a wet washcloth covering his face.

"I just talked to Mr. A, we need to get Two into bed."

Two yanked the cloth from his face and shouted.

"I need to go to the fucking hospital man."

"Let me finish, Mr. A has a doctor coming here to the house in...."

He raised his arm up and looked at his wristwatch.

"About forty-five minutes. We have to be on the move in thirty minutes, so I suggest we get back to the kitchen and go over the plan since we will now be one man short."

Two did not want to move so they brought a pillow and blanket into the bathroom for him. He lay quietly on the floor curled up in the fetal position underneath the blanket. The remainder of the team went over the plans and determined who would take over for Two.

Just as they were walking out of the house, a car pulled into the driveway. The three men watched as a tall sturdy looking fellow got out and walked up to the side door of the house with a small black bag in his hand. One pulled the door open.

"I guess you're the doctor?"

Thomas Pierce said nothing and only brushed past the men and stopped to look in the living room. Four, who stood at the doorway, spoke up.

"He's in the bathroom on the floor."

Without comment the doctor walked to the bathroom and entered closing the door behind him.

Number One shook his head as he spoke to his team, "Let's go gentlemen, we have work to do."

The three men walked to the garage and got into the large van before opening the door and pulling out past the doctor's car.

The doctor sat his black bag on the counter next to the sink. He undid the latch and slowly opened the bag as Two eyed him cautiously from the floor.

"I need something for the pain, Oxy or at least Vicodin or Percoset."

The doctor pulled his hand out of the bag and pointed the silenced Glock pistol at the prone mans chest and fired three times. He carefully placed the gun back into the bag.

"That should stop the pain."

Friday July 1, 2011

5:15 PM

Downtown Akron

Two young women wearing colorful bikini tops, the tightest of short shorts and leather sandals, leaned in close and whispered conspiratorially before bursting out in laughter. Their beer bottles clinked together as they watched the large man exit the building just across the street. He staggered slightly as the heat that radiated off of the street seemed to slap him in the face. His shirt already showed large wet stains under his arms as he adjusted the pack on his back and checked the time on his wristwatch.

A Jimmy Buffett tribute band had just finished setting up all of their equipment for the night's free downtown concert and they now launched into their sound check. The big man stood nervously on Main Street and listened to them singing about a holdup that cost them two good years and he broke into a broad smile. He checked his watch once more as three uniformed police officers walked past. Eyeing them cautiously, he adjusted his backpack and moved off in the opposite direction.

He crossed the street in front of barricades that closed off vehicle traffic as people streamed into the downtown area for the free concert that was to be followed by a dual fireworks show. The city had orchestrated with the hometown AA baseball team the

Aeros, to put on an extra special show that would kick off the long holiday weekend with a bang.

Herman "Tiny" Murphy wheezed heavily as he walked back to his vehicle His shirt was soaked with sweat by the time he made it the two blocks to his car. He gingerly pulled off the backpack before placing one meaty palm on the door and gently setting the backpack on the passenger seat. With an effort, he pulled himself up and into the front seat of the non-descript white van. He quickly inserted the key into the ignition and started the engine. He wiped droplets of sweat from his face as the air conditioning kicked into action although it did little to slow the flow of perspiration and his hand shook nervously as he watched the clock.

Between the seats was a large red and white cooler and Herman reached down and opened the lid. Pulling out a can of diet pop, he opened it and drained it in a single pull. Tossing the empty behind the seat he quickly pulled out a second can. He only took a small sip before placing it in the cup holder. The next reach towards the cooler produced a restaurant to-go container brimming full of fried chicken. A furtive glance at the clock on the dash showed that he had plenty of time for a snack. He popped open the lid and attacked the defenseless chicken with gusto.

Friday July 1, 2011

5:15 PM

Downtown Akron

The armored car from the Federal Reserve Bank in Cleveland pulled up to the curb in downtown Akron for the first of its three stops. Driver Jim Allen logged in the time of arrival as the other three members of the team moved the deposit into the bank. Six minutes later they were once more on the move.

Friday July 1, 2011

5:15 PM

North Hill area of Akron

The three remaining members of Team Fed tried to relax as they now sat in a plain white van across the street from the credit union branch. They watched as Mr. A pulled up next to the van and a woman got out and approached them. Before she had even made it to the vans sliding side door Mr. A had driven off.

As she slid the door open she smiled at the three men briefly as she stated, "I'll be number three now." Even though she wore a loose fitting one-piece jumpsuit the men all smiled back as they pictured how good she must look without it.

As if she knew where their minds were at and in an attempt to get them back on track, she began reviewing the plans with them.

The Plaza in Fairlawn

The Gold Partners Corporate Headquarters and largest store.

5:40 PM

Team Gold

The white truck with a "cherry picker" bucket pulled around the back of the shopping center and drove past several trucks backed into the various loading docks. The truck stopped about fifty feet away from the Gold Partners loading area. The loading area was closed off from traffic by a high chain link fence with razor wire stretched across its top rail. Cameras swept the area although they could not see the truck pulling up just a short distance away.

The diver's long blonde hair was pulled back into a ponytail that peeked out from under his white hardhat as he placed orange traffic cones around the truck. He put a tool belt around his waist and then pulled on what looked like a backpack except that this one had the pack in the front. He climbed up into the bucket and raised himself up along the side of the building until he was looking at a two foot square electrical box. He raised the canopy on the bucket and was now effectively hidden from view.

After snipping the wire holding the panel closed he opened it and quickly went to work. Within three minutes he folded down the front of the pack on his chest and pulled a couple of wires out and clipped them into the panel. He smiled as he watched the live feeds from the stores security cameras on the screen in front of him.

He picked up his walkie talkie, "Three ready to go."

Friday July 1, 2011

5:40 PM

West Akron

Jim Allen guided the armored car up to the curb outside of the Guarantee Savings and Loan and logged in the time as the others made the routine deposit. They were back on the move in less than four minutes and headed for their last stop at one of the smaller branches of a local credit union.

Friday July 1, 2011

5:50 PM

Gold Partners Corporate Headquarters

The Gold Partners corporate headquarters were housed in the back portion of their first and also the largest store in their chain. It was doing a brisk business with seventy to eighty people browsing the stores extensive jewelry collections and another twenty or so who stood in line waiting to turn their old gold items into some new folding green.

At the rear of the store in a windowless room sat Jermaine Orton before a bank of television monitors. He stifled a yawn as his eyes slowly moved back and forth across the screens. Each customer who entered received a glance and each time a purchase was made, both the buyer and the sales associates were watched. The cash registers always got special attention. The monitor on the far right showed a split screen with two shots of the front exterior of the building. The monitor on the far left was also a split screen with three camera shots showing the building's exterior including a gate and loading dock.

Jermaine watched as a well dressed European looking man with a thin mustache entered alone and walked to a case that featured men's watches. He carried a suit coat folded over his arm. A middle aged man and an attractive looking woman came in holding hands. She held in her hand two shopping bags from the high end dress shop next door and the couple headed toward the ring section.

A young black male was the next to enter; he wore a ball cap pulled down low over his face and a hooded sweatshirt that concealed it even more. The man's hands were hidden inside the oversized sweatshirts front pocket and his head swiveled back and forth as he bounced nervously from foot to foot. He headed toward the line for gold sales and eyed the cashier behind the Plexiglas and iron bars.

Jermaine picked up a radio.

"Marcus, eyes on the floor, end of the line."

A rapid response came back, "Copy that, I got'em."

Marcus wore a security guard uniform and walked casually over to the front of the line before turning and slowly walking past each of those in line. He stopped in front of the young man who now stared down at the floor.

"Excuse me."

He received no response. The second time he reached out and tapped the man on the shoulder as he spoke, "Excuse me."

The young man tilted his head back and smiled, "Sup brother?"

"Need you to take off your hat in the store."

The smile disappeared in an instant and he moved slightly forward while his chest puffed out, "Fuck that shit. I don't wanna do no bidness here anyway."

He turned and walked out as Marcus stood still and shook his head. Jermaine went back to his normal routine. No one took notice of the woman's shopping bag left next to one of the display cases or the men's suit coat that now lay draped neatly over a chair.

Friday July 1, 2011

5:50 PM

West Akron Mall

Officer Jack Wesley was on patrol in his cruiser when he pulled up behind a charter bus parked in a far corner of the mall parking lot noting that it was odd to see a bus sitting here. Just as he was about to approach the bus to speak to the driver, the blast of a horn sounded an instant before the crunching of metal and shattering glass interrupted him.

He drove over to the accident as he called it in over the radio.

Friday July 1, 2011

5:55 PM

K-Mart

Stanley "Sudz" Oldman pulled into the K-Mart parking lot looking to pick up some last minute supplies for his own fourth of July party the following Monday. He knew that this was his last chance to do any shopping as he would be busy all weekend tending bar at a lively club on the edge of the UA campus, hence his nickname.

His cell phone rang just as he pulled through the intersection into the lot and he pulled off into the first empty spot. He picked up the phone and began talking to one of the lovely young ladies who frequently stopped by on evenings he worked. Stanley was twenty-five years old and only a few months since his discharge from the Army.

He had been early in his second tour of Iraq when an IED had nearly taken his life. After months in rehab he was able to walk with only a slight limp to betray his attempt at normalcy.

Until he decided what he was going to do, the bartending job kept him busy and the girls kept him occupied in his off hours.

He smiled as they made small talk and he gazed absentmindedly out the window. A greenish blue van came up the aisle and Stanley tilted his head sideways while looking at the driver, the man in the passenger seat stared up at a semi-trailer that sat with its engine idling. He also saw of glint of gold reflected off of the teeth of the man in the passenger seat.

Stanley shifted his eyes to the big rig in time to see the driver lean out the window and give the thumbs up sign to the two men in the van as they passed by.

"Sorry, I gotta go."

With that Stanley snapped his phone shut and tossed it on the seat as he sat up straight. The hair on the back of his neck had stood up and a shiver had run down his spine. It had been early on his first tour that he quickly learned to listen to his own body's early warning system and it had saved his life more than once. His head swiveled side to side scanning the lot and once again he focused on the rig as it swung around in an arc and parked facing the last entrance to the parking lot on the south side. He watched as the van pulled up into the first open space closest to the store.

Stanley glanced at his watch as he waited in vain for someone to exit the van. He reached down under the seat and pulled out the locked box that held a forty-five automatic that he was licensed to carry under the state's concealed carry law. He tapped a finger on the box and slid it back under the seat.

Friday July 1, 2011

5:55 PM

Derby Downs Racetrack

As late afternoon edged into early evening the sight of the Goodyear blimp shown in the Akron sky and its familiar droning sound caused heads to turn once more as it graced the sky with its presence.

At the same time as the blimp flew over the sight of the All American Soap-Box Derby crowd, four cars followed by four tractor trailer rigs pulled out into traffic on each of the legs of the Akron Expressway. All eight vehicles reached fifty-five miles per hour and stayed in the far left lanes.

Friday July 1, 2011

5:57 PM

K-Mart

Stanley Oldman sat in his truck and alternated watching the tractor trailer rig and the van with the men. He couldn't see anything else out of the ordinary and after taking a deep breath he was about ready to write this off to paranoia and an overactive imagination. Looking at his reflection in the rear view mirror, he spoke out loud to himself.

"You're back in Akron dude, relax!"

He started to move the truck closer towards the store when he saw an armored car pull up outside the front entrance. Stopping, he glanced over to see the van bouncing slightly as someone inside apparently moved around.

Instead of parking and going into the store he parked two rows over from the van and then turned in the seat so he could again watch the armored car and the van at the same time.

Friday July 1, 2011

6:00 PM

Downtown Akron

Herman Tiny Murphy sat in the white van looking at the screen of a laptop computer that sat on the seat next to him. He watched as the clock/counter hit six on the dot and the many boxes rapidly lit up signifying that each site had indeed received the signal for detonation.

The series of explosions in multiple locations effectively cut off most cell phone communications and local 911 services were shutdown. Police and fire emergency services were left with no internal communication link. Traffic lights and signals were out in seventy five percent of the city. The city's entire emergency services computer system crashed.

The building that housed the Akron police department went dark as it lost power. Within thirty seconds the back-up generators started providing enough power to operate lighting and most security monitoring devices. The forty-four police officers who were out on patrol or already handling calls for service were effectively cut off from any centralized command and therefore on their own.

It took about five seconds before the traffic signals went out and another minute or so before car horns began honking as frustrated drivers let loose. He flipped open his phone only to get a no signal message.

Smiling, he snapped it shut and tossed it onto the passenger seat.

Friday July 1, 2011

6:00 PM

The Plaza in Fairlawn

APD officers Walker and Goodwin sat in a booth of the Chic-Fil-A restaurant finishing the last bites of their lunch, chatted about their kids and made general small talk. They were interrupted by the buzz throughout the crowd as people began complaining loudly about losing their cell phone service. Without a thought both officers reached for their own phones and after a few seconds each glanced at the other with looks of equal consternation.

Jim Walker reached to his shoulder, keyed the microphone for his radio and called in to base. When he received no response, Kimberly Goodwin tried her own radio even as they headed outside to their cruisers. The remains of their lunch lay forgotten in the call to duty.

Friday July 1, 2011

6:00 PM

The Plaza in Fairlawn

The Gold Partners Corporate Headquarters and largest store.

Team Gold

Number Three had watched as a van and an oversized pickup truck pulled up beside his own truck while he stood perched thirty feet in the air. He gave them a thumb up signal and received one in return from each of the vehicles.

He glanced at his watch and as it clicked over to six on the dot, he shut off the security cameras and killed all power into the building. Inside the van the man with the pencil thin mustache flipped a switch that sent thick black smoke billowing from both the suit coat and from the bag left inside the store.

The pickup truck blasted through the security gate and skidded to a halt outside the loading dock doors. The van pulled up right behind and five black clad figures raced up to the man door. Each had a full face gas mask perched atop their head and all wore body armor. All were heavily armed with automatic rifles and the largest of the group also held a long steel battering ram which he swung back and then launched forward. Upon impact a cylinder inside the ram fired and the door swung backwards as the team rushed through the opening.

Inside the store chaos was taking place as customers and employees scrambled to get outside through the acrid smoke and relative darkness in the interior of the building.

Jermaine raced from the video monitoring room as soon as the monitors and lights went out. He called to Marcus and the other three members of his security team to stay calm and report in.

Marcus reported the smoke in the front store area and that the panicked customers and employees were fleeing the store. The guard assigned to the office areas reported that the power was out but that everyone there was calmly heading to the exits. The guard assigned to watch the floor from behind a large two way mirror also reported on the confusion in the front of the store. The guard on duty near the main vault reported no issues and that the security lighting had come back on already.

Jermaine had made his way down the hall toward the front of the store when a resounding boom stopped him dead in his tracks. He knew that the heavily secured back door had just been breached. He pulled his weapon and radioed his team to come to the vault area and that they were under attack. He told his man at the vault to call it in and secure his area.

Jermaine Orton stood at the corner of the hallway with the safety off of his gun and the barrel pointed straight up at the ceiling. He could hear footsteps heading his way and took a deep breath.

A man stepped out into the open corridor and Jermaine lowered his weapon instantaneously. The hallway erupted in a barrage of gunfire as Jermaine dove out of sight. He looked at the wall across from him and his jaw dropped at the sheer number of bullet holes in it. He looked down at his own weapon and amid the panic and adrenalin rush all he could think of was the scene from the movie Jaws and he thought, I'm gonna need a bigger gun.

"Drop your weapon and you will not be harmed."

Jermaine listened and decided he only had one option. He swung his hand out and let loose with three or four random shots down the hallway. A tear gas canister caromed off the wall and began spraying its toxic brew in his direction. He scrambled to his feet and raced toward the front of the store.

At the vault room, the guard lay on the floor with his hands strapped together behind his back. He had quickly decided that fourteen-fifty an hour wasn't enough for this job and vowed to find other employment if he got out of this alive. He lost his train of thought as the entire building shook on its foundation and he was enveloped in a cloud of smoke and debris.

Gunfire echoed through the building and somewhere an unseen woman was alternatively screaming and crying. Smoke canisters were everywhere and everyone still inside the building feared the worst as they prayed for their lives.

Friday July 1, 2011

6:00 PM

Interstate 77 and Interstate 76

The four big rigs headed east, west, north and south and precisely at six o'clock they each began angling across all lanes of traffic until the highways were effectively closed. Each driver pulled the key from the ignition, slid over to the passenger side and climbed down to the highway as the car each was paired with, sat waiting. The four different drivers hopped in the four waiting cars and were off and headed to their designated locations only minutes away.

Friday July 1, 2011

6:00 PM

North Hill area of Akron

Team Fed

The Federal Reserve armored car pulled up in front of the credit union branch and driver Jim Allen smiled as he logged in the time as 5:59:50. He picked up the radio to call in their arrival when he was jolted back in his seat as the entire vehicle accelerated forward. Before he blacked out he thought someone had to have been going pretty fast when they rear ended them. He never felt the car tip up on its front end at almost a forty-five degree angle before dropping back down with such force that the rear axle snapped.

A white panel truck skidded to a stop at the rear of the car just as it hit the ground in a cloud of dust and smoke. Two and Four leapt out of the back while the new Three jumped out from the front passenger seat and ran to the front doors of the building where she quickly wrapped a heavy chain through the door handles and slapped a padlock through the links as a uniformed guard on the other side of the glass frantically tried to get through to his dispatcher. One, who was driving the van, stepped out with an automatic weapon and scanned the area.

The two men went into the smoldering rear compartment of the armored car and quickly located the four satchels and began rolling them out one at a time. Three wheeled them over to the rear of the van where One then easily hefted the two hundred and twenty pound satchels inside.

In less than ninety seconds all four team members were back inside the van as it sped away. Jim Allen sat behind the wheel of the now empty armored car and pressed his hands to his ears as he opened his mouth wide in an attempt to clear the ringing and pounding in his head.

Friday July 1, 2011

6:00 PM

West Akron Mall

Officer Jack Wesley waved traffic around the accident scene as a wrecker pulled one of the damaged cars up onto a flatbed. He then walked over to his cruiser as he noted the armored car pulling up to the mall's main entrance. Although he couldn't put a finger on it, he tended to pay extra attention to those armed deliveries and pickups ever since he had observed the photo taking session a week earlier. He paid no notice to the plain grey van sitting across from the same entrance.

Two other cruisers were now on the scene when one of the officers shouted over, "Lost comms, can you raise anyone?"

Jack reached in and tried unsuccessfully to contact anyone. When he straightened up he happened to glance over to see the armored car pulling away from the curb. He also caught movement from his left and saw the bus moving from its spot in the corner of the lot.

He turned away and began talking to his fellow officers about the problem with the radios.

Friday July 1, 2011

6:01 PM

The Plaza in Fairlawn

The Gold Partners Corporate Headquarters and largest store.

Smoke began billowing out the front doors of the Gold Partners store as customers raced outside screaming frantically for help. Officers Walker and Goodwin jumped in their cruisers and raced across the lot as they tried unsuccessfully to call for assistance.

The officers continued helping people from the store until the sounds of gunfire changed things entirely. They tried one more time to call in for help before Walker volunteered, "Looks like it's just us on this one."

The two checked their weapons and headed inside without another word. They found a large uniformed security guard who reported heavy automatic gunfire coming from the corporate offices in the rear of the store. The two officers nodded to each other and Goodwin headed back outside.

She threw the cruiser in gear even as she pulled the riot control shotgun from its mount and headed for the rear of the building.

Friday July 1, 2011

6:03 PM

West Akron Mall

The armored car was loaded in less than two minutes and pulling away from the curb as the charter bus pulled through the intersecting row of the lot entrance and stopped, effectively cutting off both lanes of traffic as the armored car slowed up. The grey van pulled up at the end of the lot and the side door slid open. A tall man known only as Two stepped out and walked to the rear of the van swinging the SMAW up to a firing position.

The driver of the armored car was looking in his outside mirror when he shouted, "Oh shit, we're getting outta here now!"

With that he gunned the engine and turned the wheel to go up over the curb and around the blocking bus. The front wheels had just hit the curb when an explosion caused the twelve thousand pound vehicle to roll over on its right side.

The five police officers who had converged at the scene of the traffic accident all ducked instinctively at the explosion and immediately jumped in their cruisers for the very short drive into the mall parking lot.

Friday July 1, 2011

6:03 PM

Team Fed

Team leader number One was practically bouncing in his seat, his long ponytail flopping back and forth as he tapped a rhythm on the steering wheel while the other three members of the team sat quietly smiling at each other. Four finally let out a yell, "We did it baby," and received a chorus of shouts in return. The woman who had replaced number Three as the latest member of the team responded coolly, "Keep it under control, we're not home free yet."

Two grinned, "Ooh I can't wait to start counting out the cash, gonna be sweet. How much ya think we got?"

Four answered with his eyes open wide and a huge grin on his face, "Don't know but those fuckers were mighty heavy."

One looked back over his shoulder, "That's what I'm talking about, we gonna be rich boys....and maam." Glancing back at the road he continued, "About six or seven minutes and we're at the safe house. Haul this shit in and get to counting."

Friday July 1, 2011
6:04 PM
K-Mart

The armored car guards exited the store and reentered their car as per their usual routine. The driver continued along the front of the store before turning left. The white van pulled out behind them only to turn in the opposite direction. The big rig rumbled forward pulling across both the incoming and outgoing lanes.

The armored car rolled to a stop as the rear doors of the van opened and one man stepped out.

Stan Oldman sat in his truck watching the events unfold before him and without thought pulled his forty-five automatic out of the lockbox. He watched as the man with the gold tooth known only to his companions as number One had now risen up and was taking aim with what Stan clearly recognized as a shoulder mounted antitank weapon.

Friday July 1, 2011
6:05 PM
The Mall

The front doors of the bus opened and gliding out gracefully was a man clad in black with an automatic weapon slung over his shoulder and a small pouch hanging on a belt at his waist. Larry Keller fresh from an overnight stay in the Akron-Summit County Jail now had on a black baseball cap, dark sunglasses and a bushy beard camouflaging his facial features. A hint of a smile played at the corner of his mouth as he watched the five cops jump into the four cruisers and race to his location not more than a football field away. He waited casually with his hands clasped behind his back. The line of cruisers pulled into the entrance drive and headed straight for the bus.

When they had cut the distance to the bus in half, the former bus driver swung the R5 South African assault rifle around and in one practiced motion flipped the safety off and unleashed a barrage of bullets into the radiator and engine of the lead cruiser as it slammed to a halt. He then let loose with a spray of fire that ripped the flashing blue strobe lights off the top of the police vehicle.

Upon firing his last round he popped the thirty-five round magazine out and it dropped to the ground amid the spent casings and he pulled a fresh one out of the pouch at his waist. It was inserted and he was firing once more as the second cruiser pulled at up an angle. He shredded the side of the car blowing out both the front and rear passenger side tires.

On the opposite side of the bus the last of the armored cars contents were being loaded into the van and one of the men peeked around the front edge of the bus and yelled for the bus driver. After nodding, the driver turned back to his targets and then emptied a third magazine at them as he walked backwards. He raced around the bus and jumped through the side sliding door and slammed it shut behind him.

The van flew out of the lot and raced through and around the line of cars backing up at the now non operational traffic lights. The driver was Four and his real name was Percival Samuel Taylor and he was grinning wildly as they careened around the stalled traffic. The two remaining police cruisers had backed out and with sirens wailing they followed in pursuit as the van weaved its way in and out of traffic as it fled the scene.

Jack Wesley wondered what the hell was going on as he led the pursuit.

Friday July 1, 2011

6:05 PM

K Mart

Stan Oldman watched as the SMAW fired directly at the rear of the armored car from a distance of one hundred yards. The impact pushed it six to eight feet forward and raised the rear of the vehicle three feet off the ground before it slammed back to the pavement amid a cloud of smoke.

The man hopped back into the van and in reverse it raced up to the devastated armored car. This same man was now joined by the driver of the van as they ran through the smoke and entered through the hole where the armored car's rear door had previously hung. The man who had been driving the big rig now stood watch.

Stan held his pistol in his hand and watched the action unfold. All these men were armed to the teeth and he knew he was no match for them by himself. He picked up his cell phone but couldn't get a signal. He dropped the phone as he spotted a huge uniformed man sprint past with his weapon drawn. Stan assumed he was an off duty cop working security at the store.

The man who had been driving the rig and was now on watch, spotted the cop at almost the same time and shouted over his shoulder to his accomplices inside the smoldering vehicle. He then opened fire at the running police officer.

Stan opened the door and stepped out as his practiced eye scoped out the scene and a plan of action rapidly formed in his mind. He raced forward using the other cars as cover. Automatic fire erupted and glass shattered as the lone cop dove out of sight behind a car. Stan peered around a pick-up truck and spotted the officer now pinned down behind what was left of a VW bug.

Stan rose up enough to get a clear line of sight on the man firing and took a steady aim. When the target stopped to change magazines, the recently discharged veteran of Iraq and Afghanistan fired three times in rapid succession and Willie Anderson who had spent so much time parked in this lot as he studied the stores operation, went down.

Stan dropped to the ground when the truck he stood beside began bouncing as one of the men exiting the armored car opened up on him with another automatic weapon. Glass sprayed over him and both of the front tires blew out.

The automatic fire stopped as several shots rang out. Stan looked up to see the officer now firing as he moved forward and Stan used the opportunity to race across to the next row of cars.

The two men ran from the armored car carrying large duffel bags and half wheeling and half carrying a dolly strapped with several metal boxes. They quickly tossed everything into the van as the driver and team leader Luis Reyes unloaded his weapon by spraying randomly at the rows of cars in front of him. The other man went back towards their compatriot on the ground, took one glance and knew he was gone. He then opened fire on Stan and the policeman until the driver jumped behind the wheel and threw the engine into gear. The last man turned to jump in when he was hit and dropped to the ground clutching at air as the officer fired again. The man regained his balance before stumbling into the rear of the van. Stan fired twice into the passenger window causing it to explode and then fired twice more at the driver as the van sped off behind the corner of the building.

Friday July 1, 2011

6:06 PM

Intestate 77 northbound

"Ground track to Big Air."

"Go ahead."

"Jack, we are a dead stop here on 77, you want to do a pass and check it out?"

"Roger that, changing course now. ETA 5 minutes."

The blimp had flown past Derby Downs where children from around the world came to race their cars down the famed hill in the All American Soap-Box Derby and was now almost over the downtown area when it turned to a southerly course shifting away from the crowds moving in to see the evenings baseball game and the free concert. The pilot then continued his conversation with the ground control van and its four man crew.

"Ah ground, we are noticing traffic tie ups at numerous intersections. Must be malfunctions with the control systems."

"Copy that air, ah, we are also getting zero traffic on the scanner."

Friday July 1, 2011
6:06 PM
The Plaza in Fairlawn
Team Gold

Number One jumped behind the wheel of the van as team members Four, Five and Six slammed the doors shut signifying that they were loaded up and ready to roll. Number Two got in the pickup as number Three ran over and jumped in.

The police cruiser skidded to a halt and Officer Goodwin stepped out and jacked a round into the shotgun. Four jumped back out from the passenger seat as the officer fired at him.

He spun sideways as the passenger door window shattered. He turned back and snarled as he let loose at the officer and the cruiser she stood behind. The magazine emptied and he quickly inserted another with only a momentary pause. He then unleashed another barrage at the officer who now lay unmoving on the ground.

Four sat back down in the seat and yelled at One, "Let's get outta here." They sped past the smoldering cruiser followed by the last two team members in the pickup. The long hair of Three fluttered in the breeze as they pulled out and he slapped Two on the arm, "Looks like we made it brother."

The rear window of the pickup shattered and Two slumped forward as Three grabbed for the steering wheel and tried to get his foot over onto the brake. He finally managed to get the truck to skid to a stop, pulled Two over and jumped behind the wheel. He slammed his foot down on the accelerator as he looked into the rear view mirror to see the police officer walking toward the truck and he ducked as she fired once more.

He barely felt the impact on the tailgate and rear of the cab as the powerful truck put distance between them and the officer. He looked over at Two who lay sideways with his head against the door. Blood dripped off the right side of his face and the sleeve of his right arm had already become saturated. Three reached over and tried to rouse him by shaking him slightly but he received no response.

When he turned his head back to look into the side view mirror, he felt a twinge in his neck and he reached up to touch the area. His hand came away bloody. He looked at his reflection in the rear view mirror and broke into a big grin.

Three followed the van as they sped away and he reached over and turned on the radio. The first several stations returned only static before he finally heard the voice of the man in black.

"Someday God's gonna cut you down. Someday God's gonna cut you down."

He hollered back at the radio, "Not today brother John, not today."

Crime Wave

Friday July 1, 2011

6:08 PM

Goodyear Boulevard, East Akron

The two men known as Seven and Eight pulled off the road and drove past an empty strip shopping center going down an overgrown driveway to an abandoned automotive service station with a dozen bays. Many of the windows were broken out and had been boarded up and years of accumulated spray painted graffiti covered the buildings exterior.

As their car pulled up, the door on the very first bay opened up and a tall hulking man waved them in and pulled the rope to close the door behind them.

Seven and Eight stepped out of the car and found themselves looking down the barrel of a silenced pistol. Seven took the first shot in the chest and dropped to the ground. Eight made it three panicked steps before two rounds in the lower back ended his attempted flight. The gunman casually put one more round in the back of each man's head before dragging their bodies over to an open section in the floor that former mechanics had once used to access the underside of vehicles. Stanley Kovanic unceremoniously dumped the bodies down into the blackness. He glanced down at his watch and walked over to bay three to await his next arrivals.

Friday July 1, 2011

6:08 PM

West Akron Mall

The two cruisers with Jack Wesley in front headed west on Tallmadge Avenue hitting speeds of eighty as they continued their pursuit of the van. The officers had no knowledge of the armored car robbery; they were only going after the man who had opened fire on them and the other cruisers. Neither officer could raise their dispatchers and so continued on alone.

The van headed towards the roundabout known locally as Tallmadge Circle, where eight roads intersected. A church and the local police station were located inside of the circular roadway. A fourth of July weekend celebration was already in full swing with two bands, numerous food vendors and several hundred people getting the festivities started as the van and the police cruisers approached the barricaded streets.

Several people yelled and one officer directing traffic knew at a glance and from experience that the vehicles approaching were going too fast to make the turn onto the circle and he frantically waved his arms in an attempt to alert them to slow down as they smashed through the orange and white wooden saw horses attempting to block access onto the circle.

Percy Taylor laughed maniacally as the van skidded through the turn but ultimately, gravity and centrifugal force combined to tip the van over on its side and it skipped easily over the curb. It clipped several small trees off at their bases as people scrambled in all directions. One of the tree branches impaled Percy Taylor just under his left armpit coming to rest only after it had pierced through his heart.

The van smacked into a converted motor home that now served as a traveling barbecue stand serving ribs, macaroni and cheese on a stick and corn on the cob. The rear doors went flying off as it flipped onto its roof and rolled over once more until it came to rest among hundreds of ears of corn as several bags worth of money fluttered through the air like confetti.

Mere seconds after the van had made its grand entrance to the party on the circle; Jack Wesley began fishtailing as it tried to navigate the turn. He would have been successful if not for the second patrol car that clipped him on the right rear bumper in a text book maneuver aimed at stopping a fleeing suspect. It was not so text book when it was a fellow officer who was the other driver.

The tap on the bumper was enough to cause Officer Wesley to lose control and the car flipped over onto its roof and skidded into a towering metal light pole, bending it over at a forty-five degree angle. Ever so slowly the metallic creaking and screeching sounds grew louder as the poles angle grew larger until it came crashing down across the roofs of four of the towns emergency response vehicles.

The second patrol car ended up on its side as sparks flew and one tire rolled off seeking its own course.

Friday July 1, 2011
6:09 PM
K Mart

Stanley Oldman raced back to his truck and jumped in while tossing his gun on the seat. He gunned the engine and headed for the corner of the building in hot pursuit of the armed robbers. Their van was not in sight when he rounded the corner and he raced on after them. As he rounded the corner at the rear of the building he scooped up his cell phone and tried to dial 911.

He slammed on the brakes as the van sat less than fifty yards away. Just as he looked at the phone to see a no signal notice displayed, the vans' tires began smoking as the driver peeled out. He followed a little slower this time.

He wondered if he had hit the driver with at least one of his shots. If that was true then each of the two men inside the van were wounded. The van slowed slightly before turning left and then the smell of more burning rubber filled the air as they sped away. Stan tried to stay back but still keep them in sight. As he followed them over a crest in the hill they were nowhere to be seen and he slammed on the brakes while spinning the wheel violently to the right and maneuvering the truck onto a side street. He floored it until he reached the next cross street in this older residential neighborhood.

He looked left and right seeing nothing and moved on to the next block. Moving into the intersection once again he continued looking for the van without success. He turned left and moved down the street while constantly looking back and forth as he passed each driveway.

Halfway down the street he rolled to a stop. Glancing down at the skid marks in the pavement he rolled the window down and he could smell the odor of burnt rubber lingering in the air.

The house looked much like every other in this neighborhood with tall evergreens lining the yard on two sides and overgrown hedges shielding the house from casual view. The garage attached to the house sat at the back of the drive with its door defiantly closed.

Stan drove on past the house before turning around and parking across the street where he had a decent view of the house. He tried his phone once and still didn't get a signal. He turned on the radio to find static where his favorite country station should have been. Switching over to the local AM news and weather station produced more empty air and it finally clicked in his mind that something big might be happening.

Friday July 1, 2011

6:10 PM

Team Fed Safe House

One backed the van into the driveway between two rows of overgrown hedges that blocked much of the view of the garage attached to the rear of the house. This residential neighborhood was quiet on this start to the holiday weekend.

The muscular Four jumped out and opened the garage door and helped direct the team leader as he backed it inside. The four person team piled out and with each one grinning ear to ear they began hauling the load of three leather pouches and the four satchels still strapped to their dollies into the house.

Four dropped one of the leather pouches on the living room floor and smiled leeringly at Three who had wheeled in one of the dollies. He gazed back as his eyes wandered slowly over her. As she walked past she grabbed his ass, "C'mon stud, we got work to do."

He laughed, "I love it when you talk dirty to me."

As the last of the loot was brought into the living room, One began working to open the lock on one of the satchels. Three jumped in quickly, "That's not the plan and you know we're supposed to wait for Mr. A before we dig into the cash. Let's not get greedy."

Number One puffed out his chest, "Don't be calling me greedy bitch. I don't need to take no shit from you.'

She raised her hands up in a peacemaking gesture and smiled, "Let's just stick to the plan."

The four person team stood and stared at the pile on the floor and each became lost in their private thoughts. Three broke the spell by walking back into the kitchen and opening the fridge. She then called out to the others, "Anybody for a cold one?"

They heard the sound of a can being opened and she stepped into the room sipping from a can of beer. She tossed one to each of the others and they toasted to their success.

One walked into the kitchen and turned on a radio that was mounted under the cabinets. After trying unsuccessfully to get reception he gave up and sat down at the kitchen table. Two headed off to the bathroom after telling everyone that he had to go drop the kids off at the pool. Four smiled just stood and stared lasciviously at Three.

She smiled back and casually asked, "Any idea what's downstairs?" He looked back with a puzzled expression until the light bulb clicked on inside his head and he responded slyly, "Maybe we should check it out."

She brushed past him and headed down the steps while he waited a couple of seconds before following. At the bottom of the steps she pulled a string hanging down and a bare bulb showed them nearly empty rooms with bare brick block walls.

She continued on into the next room but didn't turn on the light. She walked over to an old work bench piled with clutter and with her back to the doorway she unzipped her jumpsuit and pulled her arms free. Four stood at the doorway and whistled softly as she shimmied a little and the jumpsuit dropped to the floor.

She wore a tight fitting top, even tighter jeans and when she bent slightly to pull her feet free; a butterfly tattoo peeked out at him. Four stepped to her as she turned to face him and he froze. She held the silenced forty-five at waist height and fired twice into the center of his chest. She casually stepped over his body and headed for the stairs.

July 1, 2011

6:11 PM

Tallmadge Circle

Larry Keller raised his head up and blinked a couple of times while mentally taking a quick check for major injuries. He lay on his back in the overturned van. He looked at the duffel bag filled with part of the haul and silently thanked it for providing a cushion that kept his head from getting smashed as the van had tumbled. He glanced at the body of his bald-headed compatriot and could tell that the man hadn't been quite so lucky. Blood pooled beside his now lifeless body.

He picked up the South African assault rifle once more, hefted the duffel bag up onto his shoulder and walked out into a scene that stopped him in his tracks. He tilted his head sideways trying to make sense of what he saw before a smile crossed his face. It was only then that he came to realize that his fake beard disguise was hanging mostly off his face, so he yanked it free and tossed it aside.

The people in the crowd appeared to be dancing around and jumping in the air grasping at snowflakes. Keller laughed as a one hundred dollar bill fluttered in front of his face and landed amid the scattered ears of corn.

He kicked the corn away as people began backing away at the sight of his weapon. He walked between two tents and headed across the road. As he stepped out onto the curb, he spotted an oversized pickup truck across the street with an elderly couple attempting to climb down from the height of the cab. Oblivious to any traffic, Keller headed straight for the truck.

A local police officer shouted, "Freeze," as he was drawing his weapon.

Without hesitation, Keller loosed off a dozen or so rounds in the officers direction even as he continued on toward what was to be his new ride.

The truck owner stood with his mouth open as the armed man walked up, held out his hand and spoke.

"Gonna need your keys Hoss, gotta borrow the truck for a bit."

With that he grabbed the keys from the old man's hand and pushed him in the chest, knocking him to the asphalt. Keller then tossed the bag and his weapon onto the seat, climbed up and hopped in. He slammed the truck into gear, jumped the curb and turned left onto the circle. He turned left again and weaved his way around the sandbagged orange barrels blocking the roadway before heading south away from the circle knowing that his first test would be getting through the cops who would surely be setting up roadblocks about one mile ahead at the main intersection by the many shops and stores that included a large K-Mart.

Keller pushed the radios console buttons and was soon singing along to the blaring tune, "Good God almighty I'm a piece of work!"

As Keller was making his way from the wrecked van, Officer Jack Wesley was popping loose the seat belt latch and dropping down to the roof of his overturned patrol car. Two sets of hands grabbed his shoulders and pulled him out of the vehicle.

The automatic fire from Keller's weapon helped Wesley make it to his feet, although a bit unsteadily. As he stood clearing the cobwebs a large red pickup truck sped away south. Jack Wesley came out of his funk enough to head straight for a Tallmadge PD cruiser that sat with its lights flashing. As one of the Tallmadge officers jumped behind the wheel to take up pursuit, Jack Wesley hopped into the passenger seat.

"Let's get that bastard."

July 1, 2011

6:11 PM

Sky over Akron

"Air One to Ground; you are not going to believe this, umm, we've got a jackknifed truck blocking all lanes northbound, uh, hold on."

Then after a short pause, the reporting continued.

"There's another truck blocking all southbound lanes and two more on the I-76 legs."

"Ground to Air, uh that doesn't sound like coincidence now does it?"

"Air to Ground, we are heading northeast towards Tallmadge, we have billowing dark smoke coming from that direction."

"Roger that, we are exiting the highway and will work toward your location, over."

"Copy that Ground."

July 1, 2011

6:11 PM

Abandoned garage

Numbers Five and Six followed their directions to the letter and pulled up to the designated location on schedule as one of the doors opened as if on cue. They entered without hesitation as the door slammed down and they squinted in the relative darkness of the building's interior.

Five was walking around from the passenger side when he heard the pffft sound. He recognized the noise and silently cursed the fact the he was unarmed. The thought was gone as quickly as it had come as momentary pain exploded in his chest.

Friday July 1, 2011

6:11 PM

Team Gold

Team Gold weaved in and around the stalled traffic with One driving the van in the lead and Three following closely in the shot up pickup. Three took another quick glance over to check once more for some signs of life from Two but found none. He started to sing along with the song on the radio when over the whistle of wind through the open cab, he heard an unfortunately familiar sound.

He turned to look over his shoulder and muttered, "Shit." The police cruiser of Officer Walker was coming on fast and Three wished he would have paid better attention to all the details of the getaway plans. Two was supposed to be the driver, so he had spent his time mostly dreaming of how he was going to lay back and enjoy spending all his money. He was originally from Cincinnati and although they had driven the route from the store to their safe house, he didn't think they were going to be able to follow the previously planned course.

One had noticed the flashing lights and took a hard right turn. The van skidded smoothly through the turn as One expertly maneuvered the vehicle just as he had once run cars around the oval tracks in his youth.

The pickup went up on two wheels as Three tried to hold it through the turn. The truck side-swiped two cars heading in the opposite direction before he was able to get it back under control. The cruiser made the turn easily as it continued to cut the distance between them.

The caravan continued on through side streets, in and around traffic and through multiple intersections with the cruiser maintaining contact with the fleeing armed robbers.

Officer Walker drove as Officer Goodwin tried in vain to contact someone as to their situation. They often had to slow down in order to protect innocent bystanders while those they chased had no such constraints.

Friday July 1, 2011

6:13 PM

Tallmadge- Akron border

Keller slowed the truck as he crested the hill; then sped up as he could see no flashing lights nor hear any sirens except those far behind him. As he passed the entrance to the K-Mart, a tractor trailer sat blocking the way. Smoke was streaming up into the air and a large crowd of onlookers were gathered. He could also see that the traffic lights were out and cars were backed up in all directions while some Good Samaritan tried to play traffic cop in the middle of the intersection.

Larry Keller pulled out into the oncoming lanes of traffic and floored it as he headed into and through the intersection all the while singing along with the radio as Commander Cody told the story of that Hot Rod Lincoln.

Jack Wesley urged his counterpart behind the wheel to push it as he tried in vain to reach anyone on the radio.

Keller flew down the straight stretch of road reaching speeds of nearly ninety while weaving around the slower moving cars. He skidded sideways as he locked up the brakes and just barely avoided crashing into a line of minivans making their way into the grade school parking lot as multiple teams played little league baseball. A dense cloud of acrid smoke hung in the air as Keller pushed the truck on past the school and down a steep hill.

Jack Wesley looked up in the air to see a sight familiar to any Akronite, the blimp. He grabbed the radio and began switching frequencies, after several clicks he could hear a conversation.

"Air to Ground, heading towards Tallmadge Circle, we have smoke from there as well, over."

Jack Wesley keyed the microphone.

"Blimp pilot this is Akron PD Officer Wesley, do you copy?"

"Roger that officer."

"We are in pursuit of a red pickup heading south on 91, can you make a visual?"

"Ah, swinging around now, hold on."

"Pilot the driver is armed and dangerous, can you contact APD dispatch?"

"Negative, all comms are down, traffic signals are out all over town."

Jack exchanged glances with the driver and they both shook their heads in puzzlement.

"Air to APD, red pickup traveling at a high rate of speed south on 91 heading into the Newton street intersection."

After a short pause the pilot continued.

"Ah the pickup went left of center, ran a car off the road that crashed into a building there. He's now through the intersection and headed toward 76."

Jack keyed the microphone.

"He's probably headed for the highway."

"Air to APD, well he's outta luck there, the highway's a parking lot in all directions."

"Copy that, we need to keep on him, there are several officers down because of this guy."

"Roger that, we'll keep you posted."

Friday July 1, 2011

6:14 PM

Team K Mart

Number Four lay on his side. Two bath towels were pressed against his shoulder and taped in place with grey duct tape. A once neatly folded bed-sheet was taped on his lower back. Both of his hands hung limply off the side of the bed. His chest heaved and he groaned loudly with each labored breath. His eyes fluttered from the effort it took to look up as his partner came into the room cursing loudly.

"Fuck, fuck, fuck, we got no fucking phones."

Four attempted to take a deep breath, grunted and spoke haltingly, "Hospital, uhhhh, dying, uhhhh, ahhhhh."

Team leader One shook his head, "Man you know that ain't in the plan."

A wet guttural roar came from Four as he tried to raise up, "Gonna die without hospital."

His head slumped back down onto the blood soaked mattress and with his eyes closed he whispered, "I won't talk, I won't talk."

With that he collapsed into unconsciousness and his team leader walked back down the hall in a daze, unsure of what course of action to take. He ran cold water into the sink and splashed it on his face while he contemplated his options.

Friday July 1, 2011

6:15 PM

Abandoned garage

One and Two pulled into a bay about halfway down the length of the building. Two sat at the wheel wiping the dash and interior for any possible prints when One let out a low grunting sound. As Two turned in his seat to see what was happening, a gun flashed in front of his face. He had no time to form a thought before his life was taken away.

Friday July 1, 2011

6:16 PM

Ellet area of Akron

"Air to Ground, suspect is moving through the Ellet area now, still south on 91."

"Copy that."

"Ground, he has turned right onto Triplett."

Wesley shouted for the driver to go hard right and they skidded through the turn as Wesley relayed directions. A second Tallmadge cruiser came up behind and joined in on the pursuit.

"Just up ahead we'll go hard left and cut the bastard off."

As Jack Wesley directed the TPD cars in their chase of the suspect, the blimp droned on overhead.

"Ground, be advised the suspect is approaching George Washington Boulevard and there are about fifteen thousand people here at Derby Downs. There are patrol cars in the area."

Larry Keller roared up to the intersection noting the three cruisers parked there. At the last instant he slammed the wheel to the left, smashed through the orange and white wooden barricades that attempted to block the way and headed up the curving George Washington Boulevard. The roadway snaked up past the now unused Rubber Bowl stadium and then to the top of the hill where the All American Soap Box Derby was being held.

As Keller headed up the hill, the three officers dashed for their patrol cars. Each of the men paused for a moment as two Tallmadge Police Department cruisers flew through the intersection after the pickup. Keller pushed the pickup up the hill while the growing parade of police cruisers raced in pursuit.

The blimp hovered overhead as the derby crowd craned their necks to see it and many applauded at the mere sight of it. Four police officers stood next to their cruisers that blocked off the road at the Top Side participants entrance into Derby Downs. Everyone craned their necks towards the oncoming sirens.

Keller burst over the crest of the hill and spotted the cars blocking the road. He slammed his brakes, turned right and drove through the chain-link fence that lined the road. He now entered into the upper section of Derby Downs where men, women and children scattered in all directions as they fled for their lives.

Jack Wesley leapt from the cruiser as it skidded to a halt and half a dozen officers took up the chase on foot.

Keller smashed into a minivan, threw the truck into reverse and backed up into a pickup. He hit it so hard that the trailer holding their derby racer was knocked over on its side. Keller saw no escape but one and he smiled broadly as he gunned the engine into action.

Wesley and the other officers knew there were too many civilians running around the area for them to open fire and they watched in stunned disbelief as the pickup headed straight for the race track.

Keller grinned wildly as he skidded to a halt at the starting line and screams came from the crowd. He didn't hear the PA announcer calling for the track below to be cleared, nor did he hear the screams from eleven year old Susie Schmidt, the hometown hero who stared up at the chassis of the pickup from inside her masters' division racer.

He began smoking the tires as a deep voice from the radio sang about riding that long black train and with a scream of his own he headed down the nine-hundred and eighty-nine foot track. He reached the finish line at the bottom of the hill much quicker than the usual twenty-seven seconds of the racers and then he proceeded to plow through a small chain link fence and down an embankment. He crossed over giant cement letters that spelled out the city's name and then lost all control. The truck flipped end over end on the small airport runway that sat next to the track. The pickup came to rest upside down with Larry Keller hanging partially out of the shattered windshield. Money littered the ground and the inside of the cab of the truck. A one hundred dollar bill stuck to his bloody shirt just below his chin.

The first person to reach him was a young paramedic stationed at the bottom of the track. He placed his fingers on the man's neck to feel for a pulse that was no longer there. He could tell by the odd angle of his head that the neck was broken.

Friday July 1, 2011
6:16 PM
Team K-Mart

It had taken Tiny Herman fifteen minutes to make his way through the crowded streets as every intersection was now effectively a four-way stop. He reached into his cooler and pulled out another can of diet soda which he drained in several large gulps as he continued on.

Taking the side streets through the residential neighborhoods helped him to avoid most of the traffic congestion. He turned the corner and without notice he passed a red pickup truck with a man who watched him as he drove past.

Tiny backed his vehicle into the driveway until he was next to the house before he shut off the engine. Breathing heavily and wiping his face with a handkerchief, he rapped on the side door of the house.

He was about to knock a second time when the curtain moved slightly. A moment later he heard the lock click open and the door swung in about three inches.

A Latino looking man with a thick black mustache looked out at him. Tiny blurted out, "Mr. A sent me here."

Luis Reyes opened the door and stepped back as Tiny noted the gun in his hand and another in the waistband of his jeans. He could also see that the right side of the man's face and shoulder had many spots where he was bleeding from.

The man asked, "Are you a doctor?"

Tiny stammered, "What? No, no I'm not."

The man stepped past and closed and relocked the door before turning and shouting, "Where's Mr. A? Four is all shot to hell and he needs a doctor. Three is dead and I don't know what happened with Two."

Tiny held up his hands, "Calm down, he called me and told me to come here and wait. Supposed to be another cat coming. He said we'd know him cause he's as big as the side of a mountain. We hafta wait for this guy to show up."

"Four ain't gonna make it much longer man. This is so fucked up."

Friday July 1, 2011
6:16 PM
Team Fed Safe House

Three waited patiently at the top of the stairs until she heard the toilet flush over the sound of music now coming from the kitchen. She opened the basement door just as Two opened the bathroom door and she fired once hitting him in the throat. He fell backwards clutching at his neck in a vain attempt to get oxygen through what remained of his shattered windpipe.

The instant she had fired the shot she had turned toward the kitchen. One had instantly shoved his chair out into the hallway and she fired as it came into view. His hand swung out around the corner and he fired twice at what would have been waist height if she had been standing in the hallway. She was two steps down the stairs and only her head and hands peeked out as the two shots he had fired shattered the door three feet above her head.

She fired twice in return and heard a grunt as he pulled back out of view. Peering out around the doorframe she could see a hole in one of the kitchen cabinets and could only assume that her first shot might have clipped him. She knew that the big man would not go down easily. She popped the magazine out and rapidly inserted another.

The heavy wooden kitchen table was tipped over on its side and he shoved it out into the hallway. She fired two shots into its center and once above it and into the refrigerator. She ducked back down the stairs as several shots ripped pieces of wood off the door frame and the splinters rained down onto her.

She was taking a deep breath and readying herself to fire again when she heard the sound of breaking glass. After a moment of silence that seemed to her an eternity, she heard a familiar voice call out softly, "Angela, Angela?"

She jumped out and ran into the embrace of Frankie Tarasco. The body of One lay sprawled out on the floor, the remains from the top half of his head now decorating the wall.

Friday July 1, 2011

6:17 PM

Team K Mart Safe House

Stan Oldman sat in the truck with his pistol in his hand as he tried to control the nervous energy that kept the adrenaline rush going. He kept watch on the house while continuing to try to get a signal on a local radio station. After watching the white van back into the driveway of the house he waited only another minute and then he slowly pulled away from the curb and drove away. One block from the house he sped up and headed back to the store to alert the police to the whereabouts of the robbers.

As he pulled into the store parking lot he was shocked to find no police cruisers in sight, although several dozen shoppers, perhaps as many as a hundred stood around in clusters staring at the still smoking armored car.

Stan jumped out and raced through the crowd asking if anyone could get a cell phone signal. He spotted the tall muscular uniformed officer standing next to a cluster of people. The man was trying to get through on the working phone of one of the folks in the crowd. Stan tapped him on the shoulder and the officer half turned while tapping a number into the phone, he stopped as he recognized Stan as the man who had helped in the gun battle with the thieves. Stan spoke up first.

"I followed them to a house nearby but can't get through to anyone."

The officer handed the phone back to its owner before responding.

"Are you off duty?"

"No, I'm Army, Ranger who's home for a while. Looked like maybe you needed a hand there. Any idea what's going on?"

"Damned if I know, a few people have phones that work but 911 is out and emergency services are out. I think we're on our own for now. How far to this house?"

"Not far, maybe three or four minutes."

The officer turned around and whistled loudly to get people's attention.

"Listen folks, as you're aware, we have a serious emergency here and we need your help."

He pointed at a group of six or seven people.

"I need all of you to stand guard on this site until other officers arrive."

He turned back to Stan.

"Do you know the street?"

"Rutland."

The cop turned back to the man with the working phone who now stood with several others.

"I need some of you to head out to the road and try to flag down any officers that arrive. You need to let them know that we have headed to Rutland Street, that's where the men who did this went. You got that?"

Without waiting for a response he turned back to Stan and stuck out his hand for a quick introduction.

"Paul Grimes, I'll follow in my car, stop when we are about a block away. We'll park on opposite ends of the street."

Friday July 1, 2011

6:18 PM

Team Gold

Officer Walker had patrolled this area for several years and was thus able to make all the right moves and close the gap on those they pursued. They were headed closer towards the downtown area where numerous officers would be on duty due to the concert, the ballgame and the fireworks. He felt confident that if he could continue to push them in that direction, it would lead to their apprehension.

One continued trying to lose the cruiser that was on their tail and in so doing passed the street where the safe house awaited them. He decided to take a different route and after hitting speeds of nearly ninety on a relatively straight stretch of road, he planned on heading closer to downtown and onto the highway.

He spun the wheel hard as they careened onto Market Street and headed toward the downtown area. They went less than half a block and as they crested the hill they were met with the sight of several cruisers blocking the road ahead. One jerked the wheel to the right and accelerated as they headed onto a side street.

As their convoy turned onto this street a rumble hit their ears as the tires made their way over the old brick paved South Bates Street, better known to locals as Cadillac Hill. Everyone was jostled and jumbled around as they headed down a short distance until a ninety degree turn to the left took them to the hill.

As they crested the hill, One as the driver and Four in the passenger seat had to lean forward to see the road as it appeared that they were about to drive off of a cliff. Without hesitating he punched his foot down and they headed down the steep hill. Every few inches the bricks of the roadway were raised up about two or three inches and the vehicles bounced like crazy. Four smacked his head into the roof of the car several times and everyone braced themselves to prevent sliding out of their seats. The cargo they carried slid forward and crashed into Five and Six, smashing Five's foot in the process.

A sharp turn to the right awaited them at the bottom of the hill and One knew that at the speed they were going they would never make it. Directly ahead of them stood a construction trailer and one large plastic porta-potty in front of an old wooden telephone pole.

Sparks flew as the front bumper of the van crashed into the brick pavement when they hit the flat area at the bottom of the hill. They sailed between the trailer and the telephone pole, jumped the curb and struck the portable toilet head on. The hard shell plastic structure crumbled upon impact and its contents exploded. Blue water and the waste it contained rained down on the windshield of the truck as it continued plowing its way through some shrubs and up a small incline. It popped out onto the roadway as One turned right and headed for the highway.

Three was pounding on the brakes as the truck bounded down the hill, he could smell the brake pads burning as they struggled to do their job. When they hit the bottom he lost control and only had time to throw his arms up to protect his face before smashing directly into the telephone pole.

Officer Walker slowly drove down the brick lined roadway amid the smell of brake fluid and burning rubber. They watched as the pickup crashed while the van sped off followed by two cruisers.

Friday July 1, 2011

6:19 PM

Team K-Mart Safe House

Tiny Herman and Luis Reyes sat at the kitchen table. Tiny sat with a half eaten apple and a can of diet pop in front of him. Number One Luis Reyes sat with his eyes fixed on his watch and sweat dripped off of his forehead.

Tiny dabbed at his own face and asked, "So, um, what happened? I mean, how did you guys get shot up?"

Luis shook his head slowly, "We went in short handed but shit man, It went bad. Some cop and some John Wayne dude came outta nowhere and shot Three. He got hit right in the throat. Four took a hit in the lower back and the shoulder and its bad man."

"Were you robbing a bank?"

"No, an armored car."

Tiny's heart became taxed even more than usual as it raced faster and in as casual of a voice as he could muster, he asked, "So how much did you get?"

"I don't know, it's all still in the van in the garage. When we got here, I just brought Four into the house. I never went back out."

He stared at his watch again, "When is this guy supposed to be here?"

Friday July 1, 2011

6:20 PM

Goodyear Heights area of Akron

James Nelson sat at the table with his arms stretched out at his sides, each hand held the hand of his son and daughter and they in turn held onto their mothers hand as he led them in thanking the Lord for all their many blessings. The rare occasion of them all being together for dinner made the time special.

"May I be excused?," his son asked as he pushed his chair back from the table.

His father smiled, "Sorry, you need to help with the dishes tonight."

His wife smiled even wider, "Yes you are excused; your father will help with them tonight."

He threw up his hands and laughed, "Yes Maam, it will be my pleasure."

Two minutes later as the husband and wife stood at the sink, their son shouted in from the living room, "Dad, the cables out."

He looked over at her with his mouth open and his eyes wide, "Oh my, the world is coming to an end."

They stood laughing as their daughter walked into the kitchen, "The radio is out too!"

Shaking his head as he dried his hands, he walked over to the small radio on the counter that they often played in the mornings while they waited for that first cup of coffee to arouse them. He punched the button for first one station and then another. After four attempts at local Akron stations returned only static he tried a station from Cleveland and their whole family stood around the kitchen and listened.

"Again for those just joining us, the breaking story is happening in Akron. We are now getting some sporadic confirmation of multiple explosions across the city, traffic lights out all over Akron, no television or radio service, most cell phone services are down…."

The radio announcer had no sooner made the last statement when all four family members simultaneously pulled their own phones out and each found no signal.

James Nelson picked up his badge and weapon and headed for the door. "Looks like I am back on duty, you just stay put until I find out what's going on."

He kissed his wife and headed out the door.

Friday July 1, 2011

6:20 PM

Abandoned garage

Number Three was a short Latino man with a pencil thin mustache and with number Four, they drove slowly up to the old garage as a door opened up on the far end and a man stepped partially out and waved them in. The muscular bearded Four muttered softly.

"Slow down."

Three turned with a puzzled expression.

"Why? This is the place Mr. A told us to drop the car."

"I'm just naturally cautious."

Four then pulled a .38 special out of his pocket and held it in his lap. Three's eyes went wide as he shook his head.

"Shit man, there's supposed to be no weapons on this job!"

"Shut up and drive in slowly so we can check this guy out. My name's Tom Burton but everybody calls me Bear."

"Supposed to be no names man!"

The doorman waved them in impatiently and the car rolled to a stop halfway through the door. Four, in the passenger seat leaned down, his hands concealing the weapon in his lap as he spoke.

"Listen, where's our ride outta here?"

The large man had to bend over at the waist in order to look into the car and he snarled.

"Get inside if you want to get paid."

Three looked over at Four, shrugged his shoulders and pulled the car forward. Before the car had come to a stop Four had stepped quickly from the car with the gun down at his side and hidden from view. Instead of approaching the man he walked backwards towards the front of the vehicle.

The behemoth of a man walked up to the driver's door as Three slid out and Four passively watched. The oversized man's left hand rose and Three fell backward, his arms flailing wildly for a handhold. Four had the Saturday night special up and got one shot off before the big man could react. The pistol shot echoed loudly through the mostly empty confines of the old garage sounding even louder in contrast to the muffled sound of the silenced weapon of their attacker.

The giant man spun slightly to the right after being hit with Four's shot. After a moment's hesitation he emptied his weapon in the direction of the man he only knew as number Four. As his last round was fired, he crouched down and popped the empty magazine out and inserted another in a well practiced motion.

Four now lay flat on the ground and fired three quick shots underneath the car. A scream followed by a mad roar told him the man would not be dancing with the stars anytime soon. Glass from the car windows exploded and showered down upon him followed by at least two shots that ricocheted off the ground and rattled under the car. He rolled over behind the front tire and searched for a way out, assuming negotiations to be out of the question.

A couple of rusty old metal wire racks bounced over the top of the car and a piece clipped the back of Four's leg. He dropped to one knee and felt blood running down into his sock. He put his left hand down for balance as he prepared to sprint a few steps to get behind the back wall of the shop when his hand grasped hold of a bunch of rusty old nuts and bolts.

He swung his hand up and let fly with its contents in the direction of his foe as he raced for cover. He thought that he heard something that resembled a muffled groan but, had no way to know for sure.

Two bays over the big man knelt down on one knee, his left hand rubbing his eyes. One of the bits of metal had hit him in the corner of his right eye. He blinked furiously as his rage grew. He simply ignored the bullet wound in his right shoulder. His right foot was pulsing blood out from the missing top section of his shoe where another bullet had ripped through the metatarsal bones. He looked down at his foot, blinked a couple of times to help clear his vision before standing up. Swaying unsteadily and breathing heavily, he began moving after this last man.

Friday July 1, 2011

6:21 PM

Team Gold

Number One spun the steering wheel hard to the right and the van turned onto the ramp that would lead them onto the MLK highway and from there only a short distance to Interstate 76. Two cruisers had now joined the pursuit and One yelled for the members of his team to get ready to open fire on them.

He pulled the van quickly off to the side of the road as the cruisers pulled up behind them and stopped side by side where they parked at a slight angle. As the officers jumped from their cars, the rear doors of the van opened and automatic gunfire erupted. Four slipped out of the front passenger seat, came around the side of the van and walked straight at the officers while they were pinned down. His eyes were wide open and a wide maniacal smile played across his face.

The cruisers jumped and bounced as the rounds pierced through them and their tires exploded.

Friday July 1, 2011

6:22 PM

Abandoned Garage

Tom Burton crouched down behind the interior wall that ran the length of the shop with openings after every other bay. He listened intently for any sound and heard only the pounding of his own heartbeat. Taking a deep breath and bending over at the waist, he ran past the first gap as quietly as he could. Nothing happened and he continued on to the next opening. Here he waited once more as he strained to detect any sound.

He moved on in this fashion until he was halfway through the garage and still no sound came back. He figured the man was either lying on the floor bleeding to death or out in the darkness waiting for him to make a mistake. He hoped for the former but planned for the latter.

Burton had just moved past another gap while looking back and forth when he tripped and fell. He threw out his hand to break his fall on the concrete floor and the gun skittered across the floor. He raced on hands and knees to retrieve it. Diving for it he rolled over on his side expecting an attack that did not come. As he looked behind him, he saw two legs sticking out from the darkness. Crawling back to the body he pulled on the jacket and the body rolled over. He recognized the man as number One from one of the other driving teams and assumed that all the others were dead or at least that had been the plan until he had come along.

He decided to move out into the front section of the garage and make a run for it.

Friday July 1, 2011

6:22 PM

Team Gold

A police cruiser pulled off to the side of the road some two hundred yards back behind the two cruisers and the officers who hid behind them as three assailants unloaded unmercifully on them. Forty-one year old Pete Whitney calmly walked to the trunk, reached inside and pulled out his department issued sniper rifle. He took two slow deep breaths as the scope honed in on the van ahead. He could make out two sets of muzzle flashes coming from inside of the van. For now he disregarded the man standing in the open just to the right of the vehicles.

The veteran officer and SWAT team leader exhaled calmly as he pulled the trigger sending the 7.62 NATO round toward his target at twenty-six hundred feet per second. One quarter of a second later the gunfire coming from inside the van stopped.

Pete Whitney's sight moved to the man standing in the open and firing at the two officers pinned down behind their cruisers. The man responded to him and sprayed a swath of automatic fire in his direction.

Once more he let out a slow breath and fired one clean shot. The man known to his companions as number Four had his two hundred and fifty pound frame lifted up off the ground and slammed backward as the two and three-quarter inch round tore through the base of his throat, less than half an inch above the top of his body armor.

The van pulled away from the scene in a cloud of black and grey smoke as the tires left behind a reminder of their passing. One as team leader and the driver had now lost any sense of confidence that they would be able to make their escape from this situation. He knew that Six was badly wounded in the back of the van and assumed that Four was dead after watching him drop to the ground.

Five, the lone woman on the team managed to pull the rear doors closed just as another round pierced through the metal and slammed into the back of the passenger seat. She threw herself flat on the floor and crawled forward.

Just as she was set to crawl up into the front passenger seat next to One, another round came through the left rear window and passed between them. It punched a hole in the windshield. One slid down in the driver's seat as Five plopped down beside him doing her best to pull her head down into her shoulders like a turtle trying to get into its shell.

Friday July 1, 2011

6:25 PM

Abandoned Garage

The muscular bearded man who resembled his nickname of Bear crouched down as he crept forward, now moving out into the bays in the front of the garage. He stopped as he thought he could make out the sound of labored breathing. He approached cautiously to find the large man sprawled out on the floor with his back against one of the overhead garage doors. An ever widening pool of blood glinted blackly at his feet. His hands lay on the floor at his sides as the pistol sat in his lap. The big man's head hung limp with his chin resting on his chest. Blood ran down the side of his face and dripped onto his shirt.

Bear reached down and swiftly plucked the gun up and in one motion tossed it down into the open oil changing pit. The man never moved except when his chest heaved as he coughed up some blood and even then his eyes never opened. Bear bent down and picked up a steel bar that stood leaning against the wall and swung it sideways. It caught the side of the man's injured foot and he let out a wet muffled scream.

"Ohhhh, sorry about that. I'll bet that stings like a bitch."

The big man looked up, blinked a couple of times and smiled.

"Fuck you!"

Bear laughed,

"I gotta give it to you, you're one tough mother. You probably like pain, so what the hell."

The piece of steel was lifted up and then dropped directly down on top of the shattered bones of the man's foot. The man rolled over sideways until his head hit the floor and once more he lay unmoving.

Bear stepped closer, pulled his foot back like a place kicker ready to kick the game winning field goal. His forward motion was aimed at the blood soaked gunshot wound in the man's shoulder. As his foot reached its intended target, the wounded giant wrapped both of his arms around Bear's ankle and rolled forward.

Bear was pulled off of his feet and slammed to the cement. The gun slipped from his hand and disappeared into the darkness as he tried to kick free from the man he had previously thought to be near dead. Bear yanked his right knee upward pulling his foot free before slamming it back into the face of the bloodied man, who only bellowed loudly and leapt forward landing on top of him.

Bear was a strong man but gave up a foot in height and maybe one hundred pounds to his opponent who now had his enormous hands encircling his neck. Bear was amazed at the strength of the man whose fingers began to dig deeper into his flesh as he struggled to free himself.

The two men half rolled to the right and then back to the left. Their momentum rocked them over and Bear found himself on top for only an instant as they tumbled once more. Bear felt a weightlessness as the two men fell into the oil change pit while locked in each other's death grip.

As they hit the bottom Bear heard the larger man's neck snap loudly even as his body cushioned Bears own fall. Bear rolled over coughing and gasping for breath only to find the lifeless eyes of a man he had only briefly known as number Six staring back at him.

Friday July 1, 2011

6:25 PM

Safe House

The red pickup stopped at the corner where Frankie Tarasco and Angela sat and watched for five minutes before they approached what appeared to be an abandoned house at the end of the street. He pulled into the drive and then backed up to an oversized pole barn. The door on the barn rose up, the truck entered and the door swiftly closed again almost appearing as if the barn had swallowed the truck whole.

Frankie backed up past a black limousine, two red minivans and one panel truck until he reached a work bench mounted to a dividing wall. Angela was out of the passenger seat and threw her arms open as Emily ran to her.

"Mom," she whispered in her ear, "I've been so worried."

Angela hugged her tighter in response and Frankie shouted, "We've still got work to do."

Frankie had the tailgate open and was pulling the first wheeled dolly down out of the truck bed when Emily jumped on his back, "Yes sir Mr. A, yes sir."

Angela shook her head, "Obviously she takes after you."

Frankie shook his head but a smile did come as he pulled another satchel out and dropped it to the floor. By the time he had pulled the last one off of the truck, all but one had already been wheeled around the dividing wall where Emily was in the process of using an acetylene torch to cut the locks off each of the satchels.

Frankie gave Angela a nod as he walked to the minivan whose rear windows were plastered with soccer ball decals lettered with girls' names. He paused to check his cell phone and with a smile he calmly put the phone back into his shirt pocket.

"I'm headed to Gold house now, then Mall and K and I'll see you girls later."

Friday July 1, 2011

6:26 PM

Abandoned garage

Number Four, AKA Tom Burton, AKA Bear, rolled over onto his back and moaned loudly as pain shot out from his shoulder. He slowly rose up to a sitting position until he felt something warm running down his back and soaking into his shirt. He reached over and began searching through the dead man's pockets. The only thing he found was a simple triangular paper clip holding a wad of bills which he stuffed into his pocket. He could find no wallet or identification, not that he had really expected to anyway.

His first attempt to stand ended as he collapsed back across the other man's legs. His hand felt something odd near the man's ankle and he smiled as he pulled the gun from its hiding place and stuffed it in his back pocket.

He rose to his feet and wobbled a bit until he regained his balance. Gingerly he reached his left hand into the front pocket of his jeans and pulled out a pack of matches. Even this minor movement caused a sharp knifelike pain to shoot out in all directions from his shoulders.

He lit a match and held it up while searching around for the way out of the oil change pit. Spotting an old trash barrel, he tossed the match in and in only seconds the material had caught on fire and lit up the area. He could now make out the stairs at the back of the room and made his way up.

Now his ankle began sending pain signals that began to push those from his shoulder into the background. Bear paused after making it to the top step, closed his eyes and blew out a deep breath. He shuffled slowly to the front of the garage and without hesitation he turned to the right and headed down toward the opposite end of the garage.

Backed into the very first bay was a black SUV that he hoped had belonged to the dead giant. He pulled the release on the side of the garage door and with a slight tug it shot upward until slamming to a stop as dirt, dust and debris rained down. His heart alternatively rose when the door opened and sank when he saw no keys hanging down from the ignition. It took a great effort for him to climb up into the seat. A small white towel sat upon the center console and when he picked it up, the key stared back at him.

His left hand lay limply in his lap as he started the car. He reached back across his body and pulled the door shut. A glance in the rearview mirror showed a dirty, grimy, blood spattered visage numbly staring back. He took the towel and wiped it across his face as he leaned back in the seat. He sat and pondered where he was going to go now when his eyes fixed upon the GPS unit mounted into the dashboard.

He reached out and coaxingly touched a finger to the unit and it sprang to life. A woman's pleasant

British sounding voice directed him to turn left onto Brittain Road and he smiled.

"Yes darling, take me home."

Friday July 1, 2011

6:30 PM

Team Nitro

Frankie tried various stations on the radio as he drove and smiled as he found only static on several local ones. He tuned to a Cleveland station and listened to their report.

"This is WMJZ radio in Cleveland, Ohio and we have this developing story. Apparently several explosions were reported in the Akron area, cell phone service is out in much of the city, 911 phone systems are down, traffic control systems are also non-functional and numerous radio stations based in the Akron area are now off the air."

"Again these reports have not been officially confirmed although we have had callers who are reporting numerous problems including....one moment please, several fires and a massive tie up on interstates 77 and 76. Well folks, it looks like a crazy start to the Fourth of July weekend. Stay tuned for more details."

Friday July 1, 2011

6:30 PM

K Mart

James Nelson had the small blue flasher stuck up on his dashboard as he pulled into the K Mart parking lot and as he stepped out of the car he was immediately surrounded by a dozen people all talking at once. He held up his hands and quieted everyone down before choosing one person to start first.

It took him five minutes to get a grasp on the situation and a few more minutes to hand out assignments to his new acting force of civilians before he headed off to find the officers who had followed the perpetrators to a house on Rutland Street.

Friday July 1, 2011
6:32 PM

Bear drove on, grimacing as the big SUV rode over an uneven set of railroad tracks. He spotted a pharmacy up ahead and pulled in to the parking lot. He took a few moments to clean his face a little better before heading into the store. He was thankful for the shopping cart so that he could use it to lean on as he bought some extra strength pain reliever, a couple of ice packs and some items to clean and bandage his wounds. He grabbed a couple of Tee-shirts and tossed them into the cart. His shirt was sticking to his back and his right sock was wet from blood running down his leg. Aches and pains came from his shoulder, the back of his head and neck and his right ankle being the most prominent.

He pulled onto a side street and drove until he spotted a closed business and pulled into the darkest area of the parking lot. He swallowed several pain relievers as the first step. It took an effort to pull his shirt off and he poured some peroxide down over his shoulder. He bandaged himself as best he could, pulled on one of the new shirts and headed out for some payback.

Crime Wave

Friday July 1, 2011

6:35 PM

Team Gold Safe House

One drove the shot up van onward with a subdued number Five in the passenger seat. They both remained silent as he followed a circuitous route through side streets trying his best to maintain both the speed limit and a calm demeanor. They pulled into the driveway of a small bland house among a street filled with virtually exact duplicates. Each had a small two car garage attached to the house. Each drive seemed to be lined with overgrown hedges or rows of evergreens and most of the yards were separated by a variety of fences.

Once inside the garage with the door closed, they walked around to the rear of the van and opened the doors. As the door swung outward it left a trail of bloody droplets in an arc on the cement floor and the congealing blood found an avenue of escape past the door latch and a small steam dribbled over the bumper.

One grabbed number Six by the ankles and pulled his body out onto the floor. There was a huge hole in the center of his chest which his heart had used to pump the full supply of his blood out into the back of the van. He pushed the body to the side and reached back in for the bags holding their take from the robbery. Five stepped up into the van and handed the bags out. These were stacked up against the garage door.

Five tried to wipe the blood off of her shoes but still left bloody footprints on the bare cement floor as they carried the bags into the house.

When the last of the bags had been deposited on the kitchen table, Five blew out a deep breath and let her shoulders sag as she stared at number One and simply stated, "That was messed up."

One looked back at her with his old boxers' battered face and replied without emotion, "We made it and that's all that matters. Gotta forget the rest. We're not outta this yet."

She looked from him to the table and then back to him, "So why don't we start counting this up and see what we got. Once Mr. A gets here, I don't plan on hanging around any longer than I have to."

Friday July 1, 2011

6:45 PM

Bear listened as his GPS mistress instructed him to turn right and proceed to the destination on the left. He paid scant attention to the two men standing in the street and talking to a man in a car on the left as he turned the corner. He reached down and pretended to fiddle with the radio as he passed them by. He ignored the voice instructing him to turn at his destination and cruised past the house. At the end of the street he turned left.

He had pegged them as cops immediately with only a glance out of the corner of his eye and was fairly certain that the guy inside the car was in uniform. He would now go under the assumption that the house was under some kind of surveillance.

Taking another left at the corner, he was now one block over from his destination. He drove slowly along while scanning for cops or even nosy neighbors but saw none.

He eased to a stop in front of two houses with for sale signs fighting a losing battle against the overgrown and weed infested front yards. Plywood covered a couple of windows on the first house and after waiting for a minute that seemed much longer, he backed up the driveway.

Bear stretched awkwardly as his body was beginning to stiffen up on him. He walked into the backyard and looked back at his destination house just behind him and only one house over.

Friday July 1, 2011

6:47 PM

K Mart Safe House

Bear had to rest the weight of his body on the chain link fence for a few moments before he could then roll himself over it. He found himself standing behind a garage whose windows had been spray painted over from the inside. He slowly made his way down the side of the structure until he came to a door. He could make out the shape of a van in the dark interior and was about to continue on toward the house when he stopped and peered in for another look. Upon closer scrutiny he could make out broken windows and at least a couple of bullet holes in the vehicle and he smiled.

After a glance back at the house he threw his weight against the old wooden door and it popped open easily as the rotted frame gave way. Bear quickly stepped inside and closed the door.

Looking in through the shattered passenger window he saw blood on the seat. He reached inside and released the door locks. Once he slid the door open the interior light lit up a chaotic scene.

There were tools, handguns, automatic weapons and some sort of bazooka looking device scattered among several bags that looked like money handling bags from a bank.

Picking one of the bags up, he quickly unbuckled the leather straps on it. A slow whistle came from his lips as he looked at the banded stacks of bills inside.

Friday July 1, 2011

6:48 PM

K Mart Safe House

Thomas Pierce had stayed at the Mall Safe House for thirty-five minutes before deciding that no one was coming and he had headed off to the K Mart Safe House. He pulled into the driveway, got out of his car and walked calmly up to the side door of the house. He tapped on the glass pane of the door with thin leather gloved hands that seemed grossly out of place on a warm July evening. His button down shirt hung down low and covered the bulges at his waistline and the small of his back.

One peered out cautiously from behind the curtain and slowly opened the door as Tiny stood anxiously beside the kitchen table. One stepped back as the tall man he had met earlier as "The Doctor", walked past. The man ignored him and aimed a question directly at Tiny instead.

"So what's the status here?"

One stepped forward, "I'm the team leader here. He just got here and he don't know nothing."

The tall man threw him a hint of a smile, "Where's the rest of this team that you're leading?"

"Four is the only one left and he needs a doctor bad. He took a couple of hits. What happened with Two anyway?"

Without comment the tall man turned and walked down the hall as One and Tiny glanced at each other and followed.

Friday July 1, 2011

6:48 PM

K Mart Safe House

Thomas Pierce walked into the bedroom, took one brief look at the blood soaked man dying on the bed and pulled out a pistol and fired two shots into his chest. There was no silencer on this weapon and it echoed loudly in the nearly empty house.

One was just stepping into the room when he yelled, "What the fuck." He began to pull a forty-five automatic out of his waistband but it never got free of his jeans before the first of two quick shots hit him at the base of his throat.

Tiny Herman scrambled back down the hallway knowing that he couldn't outrun his team Nitro mate. He stopped in the kitchen and stood his ground trying to appear calm even as the stains under his arms grew ever larger.

Tiny had known Frankie Tarasco for almost twenty-five years and refused to believe that this would be his end. Pierce walked into the room and placed the gun on the table. He looked at Tiny and casually asked, "Where is the take from the job?"

Tiny knew that it was still in the van in the garage and briefly tried calculating the odds of giving a false story to this stone faced killer and decided against lying to him. Tiny glanced over his shoulder and blurted,

"Garage, he said it was still in the garage, still in the van."

K Mart Safe House

6:48 PM

At the sound of the first two shots from inside the house, Detective Nelson pointed at the officer who had been on duty inside the K Mart store, "Grimes you come with me, we'll go up the drive," he pointed at Stanley, "You watch the front."

He switched the safety off on his service pistol and trotted off toward the house with the officer on his heels. They were approaching the front corner of the house when two more shots rang out and they stopped momentarily.

James Nelson began moving once more as Officer Grimes followed diagonally across while watching the windows of the house for any movement. Stan Oldman knelt down behind a parked car in the street and kept his weapon trained on the front door.

Friday July 1, 2011

6:49 PM

K Mart Safe House

Thomas Pierce grasped the handle on the glass sliding door and whisked it open. He paused and pointed out the door indicating to Tiny that he was to lead the way. Tiny Herman reluctantly pulled the curtain aside and stepped out into the early evening heat that hit him once more like a blast furnace.

His sweat glands kicked their production into high gear and not only from the heat as he nervously waited for a bullet to the back of his head. His foot wavered in mid air at the top step when he heard the word "Freeze", shouted from the driveway and he did.

The sound of gunfire coming from behind him spurred him to hastily scamper down the steps where he promptly belly flopped onto the overgrown grass of the backyard. He tried to crawl away from the back and forth of more gunshots than he cared to count. Tiny made it as far as the remnants of a child's swing set when he let out a howl and futilely attempted to reach a meaty paw around to his rear.

He knew the stinging pain wasn't from a wayward bee and as the blood began flowing freely down the side of his hip he mercifully passed out.

Pierce had emptied a total of fourteen shots toward the cops in the drive. Almost simultaneously he popped the magazines free from each of the weapons and quickly had new ones inserted. He moved quickly down the steps and across the yard. He never hesitated as he hit the door on the side of the garage with his shoulder. He expected it to give with some resistance but it swung inward with little contention.

He jumped into the front seat and smiled as his fingers found the keys hanging from the ignition. Holes began appearing in the garage's front windows although the heavy old wooden door panels stopped most of the incoming fire.

He took a quick glance over his shoulder but could not ascertain if the take was in the vehicle or not but this was now about survival, not money. He pushed the remote laying on the dash, turned the key and once more smiled as the engine roared to life. In his left hand a forty-five automatic hung outside the window as he threw the transmission into gear and slammed his foot down on the accelerator.

James Nelson and Officer Grimes both opened fire as the van pulled out of the garage and immediately made a left turn into the backyard. The tires spun grass, weeds and dirt into the air as they dug for traction. Tiny Herman never felt the tires go across the back of his skull as the swing set bounced off the front bumper and toppled over on its side.

The van hit the decorative wooden fence and sent pieces flying in all directions. A barbecue grill and plastic chairs were flung aside as Pierce spun the wheel back to the right and headed down the empty driveway.

Stanley Oldman stood calmly near the curb and aimed into the front windshield. He fired three times before jumping sideways behind the thick tree trunk that he hoped would save him from the imminent collision.

Stanley braced himself for a crash that did not come. He looked up as the van instead rolled across the street and rammed into a large SUV. The rear doors of the van hung open and a trail of debris marked its trail down the drive.

James Nelson ran up to the driver's window, took one look and lowered his weapon. A bullet had hit the driver in the forehead and much of what had once been his cerebral cortex covered the interior of the van.

Friday July 1, 2011

6:50 PM

Team Gold Safe House

One shook his head from side to side and with his eyes closed he softly said, "One point two and some change."

He opened his eyes and stared at the stacks of cash piled on the table. Five smiled back as she looked up from the two satchels at her feet, "I'm guessing we got at least a couple hundred thousand worth of gold and no telling about all these diamonds and gems. We may be in the neighborhood of two mil."

One grinned, "And that's a nice neighborhood."

Friday July 1, 2011

6:52 PM

Frankie Tarasco took his time moving through the side streets and did his best to avoid the traffic tie ups that were in place at most intersections. He passed two police cruisers and the officers who were trying to clear up a multiple car accident.

He headed down a nearly deserted side street in a quiet neighborhood and the slight smile on his lips disappeared rapidly as he slowed the minivan down to a crawl. He stared at the van that was now t-boned into an SUV just outside of the K Mart Safe House. Two men stood in the street and although neither wore a uniform, Frankie knew without a doubt that they were cops.

He sat now in the unmoving vehicle and stared down the street until one of the men turned and began staring back at him. Frankie lifted his foot off of the brake pedal and slowly moved off.

Friday July 1, 2011

6:57 PM

Gold Team Safe House

Frankie drove in silence through more relatively quiet streets and noted that it seemed as if many more people than usual were out in the front sidewalks talking to each other on this evening.

He stopped the minivan at the corner, watched and waited for any suspicious activity. When none was forthcoming, he pulled away from the curb and pulled up in front of a house that was virtually indistinguishable from any of its neighbors. He sat quietly for another minute before slowly backing up the driveway. He stopped the minivan with the side door directly across from the door of the house and got out.

As he stepped up to the door the curtain moved slightly and he froze in place. He dared not take his eyes off of the door although he kept the gun in his hand down at his side and thus out of sight of whoever was in the house. He heard a vehicle drive past but did not turn around.

A click signified the lock being opened and the door swung inward. One motioned for Mr. A to enter and he did so without comment.

Friday July 1, 2011

7:00 PM

Gold Team Safe House

Bear sat parked in the SUV along the curb with several other cars and trucks and wondered what action he should take. He had no doubt that it was Mr. A that had pulled up to the house and then backed up the driveway. He watched Mr. A standing in the driveway of the house the GPS had directed him to.

He was also certain that Mr. A deserved some payback. Now all he had to do was figure out the when and where and how.

Friday July 1, 2011

7:02 PM

Gold Team Safe House

Frankie slipped the weapon into his pocket as he stepped inside the house. One, the team leader silently wore a look of concern and Five also stared at him wordlessly. Frankie looked from one to the other and decided to cut short the awkward silence.

"Where are the other team members?"

One shook his head slowly, "They're all gone. Six's body is out in the garage, the rest didn't make it."

Five stepped toward Frankie, "It was fucked up and all I want to do is get the hell out of here. So let's settle up and I'm on my way."

Frankie nodded his head in the affirmative as she spun on her heel and marched into the living room. Frankie put his left arm around the shoulder of his team leader and they followed after Five.

"We took the liberty of counting it out," Five stood next to the coffee table where the take had been placed.

Frankie pointed at the stacks of cash, "How much here?"

Five responded casually, "One point two and some change."

Frankie looked at the remainder of his team and matter of factly stated, "Divide the cash into thirds and I will take the gold and jewels."

The woman glanced at One for the briefest moment before they both began separating the stacks into three piles. They both placed their hand on the same stack when the team leader spit blood from his mouth and dropped to his knees.

Five sat back on the couch and shook her head. The first of two bullets tore through her chest cavity and she slumped sideways onto the cushions. Silently she stared at the piles of money as she slipped into unconsciousness.

Frankie picked up the satchels and shoved the money back inside of them. He hoisted them over his shoulders and headed out of the house without a look back.

Friday July 1, 2011

7:05 PM

Gold Team Safe House

Bear sat smiling as he watched Mr. A pull out of the driveway. He waited for his former boss to make it to the end of the street before he then pulled away from the curb and followed after him.

He kept a fair distance back to avoid detection and as a result almost lost him a couple of times. Fortunately Mr. A was driving slowly and carefully so as not to attract any attention to himself and that made him an easy mark.

Bear silently questioned whether he should just take the money he already had and call it a night or continue on with this mission of revenge.

A pothole in the road jarred the big SUV enough that it sent a lightning bolt of pain through his shoulder and up his leg. That proved enough to tip the scale in favor of payback. He figured the other poor bastards that had been killed for no real reason would also appreciate some measure of retaliation.

Friday July 1, 2011

7:15 PM

Safe House

Bear watched as Mr. A drove his minivan up the drive and into a large barn behind what appeared to be an abandoned house. He drove past slowly and as the large door rolled up he caught a glimpse of someone standing to the side as it opened and closed. As the door rolled back down the figure turned and walked away and from the sway of the hips Bear knew that it was a woman.

Bear stopped one house away and pulled into a spot between two other vehicles. He sat and as he rolled his shoulder in its socket trying to loosen it up, his mind drifted off.

He pictured his old high school wrestling coach. The crew cut and the flat nose would come within an inch of his young charges faces as he screamed at them. They dared not look away as spittle flew from his lips. "No pain, No gain ladies," he would roar constantly in a mantra that was filled with other equally trite platitudes.

Bear looked in the rearview mirror and smiled as the image of coach glared back in a rage as he bellowed, "We didn't come this far to lose ladies, No pain, No gain."

"Damn straight coach, damn straight," he replied as he opened the door and stepped out into the street. He ignored the pain that shot forth from his ankle and the adrenaline once more rushed through his system as he headed up the driveway using the overgrown hedges as cover.

He made it to the front of the large pole barn and found that the windows in the large roll up door that had appeared dark from the street had in fact been painted over with black paint from the inside. He could only make out a glimmer of light from inside.

He looked down the side of the garage and saw nothing but some stacked firewood and so made his way across the front of the garage. About six feet down the right side of the barn he came to a door whose window had been similarly painted dark from the inside. Sitting off to the side of a small brick walkway was an old barbecue grill that now sat rusting in neglect. Hanging from the side of the grill were a set of tongs, a wire brush and a long flat spatula.

Bear took the spatula and wiped some of the rust off its flat surface and stepped up to the door. Slowly he placed his hand on the doorknob and gave it a turn to no avail.

He slid the spatula blade in between the door and the frame and pushed gently against the lock until it clicked open. He tossed his impromptu lock picking device into the grass and pulled out his weapon.

Taking a deep breath he pushed the door open and braced for the inevitable barrage of gunfire but, none came. Stepping in quickly, he closed the door quietly behind him and using the vehicles in the large barn as cover, made his way to the rear.

A light whirring noise came to him among some muted voices. A woman's laugh rose above the other noises in the rear of the barn that was separated by an interior wall about three quarters of the way back. A man's voice spoke but Bear couldn't make out any words. The buzzing, whirring noise stopped and he could clearly make out two female voices and the word, "Mom."

Bear stooped down behind the van closest to the door he had just entered as footsteps came around the wall on the opposite side of the barn. He watched Mr. A carry two small suitcases over to a red minivan that sat with its rear hatch open. Mr. A placed them into the back of the minivan and moved out of sight as he returned to the rear of the barn.

Bear stepped over to the minivan and smiled as he saw six identical suitcases lined up in a row. He leaned in and smiled once more as he spied the keys hanging down in the ignition. He moved slowly toward the voices in the back with the gun in his hand leading the way forward.

He stood at the edge of the wall that divided the garage-barn into two sections and listened to the muffled voices of the man and the two women. He finally figured out what the whirring sound was as stacks of bills of various denominations were counted out, stacked and banded like so many decks of cards.

He took a deep breath and heard the old coaches refrain ringing in his ear, "We didn't come this far to lose ladies."

Tom Burton stepped out into the clear and fired one shot into the back right thigh of Mr. A who dropped to the floor with a moan and clutched at his leg. The two women both jumped up and Bear got off two shots at Angela as she reached for a gun on the workbench near her. The second shot hit her in the right shoulder and she screamed as her body slammed back into a stack of boxes and she slumped to the cement floor.

Emily raised her thirty-two caliber pistol but was never able to fire a shot before her knee exploded in pain. The gun spun unnoticed from her hand as she joined both of her parents in writhing on the floor in pain.

Bear looked from one to the other as each of the three lay in their own ever expanding pools of blood. He stood quietly as each one grew still and silent. He walked over to the ringleader and used his foot to push a forty-five automatic away from Mr. A's prone body. He raised his arm and pointed his weapon at the back of the man's head for a full ten seconds before lowering it. He felt that the man's breathing was shallow and would die soon anyway. He turned to walk away, looked back and threw a kick into the man's side. The man responded with little more than an umph sound as he slipped back into darkness.

Bear walked over to the workbench and grabbed the remaining neatly stacked cash and tossed it into another of the identical suitcases. He picked up two more pistols and tossed them into the case before closing it up. He walked back to the minivan and sat the suitcase in amongst its brethren and slammed the rear hatch closed. He opened the driver's door and started the engine and pulled forward to the door.

Leaving the engine running, he picked up his gun and got out of the van. He walked back past the wall and froze in his tracks. The bodies of all three were now gone. Three trails of blood merged into one and led to the rear of the barn and Tom Burton silently cursed himself for not finishing them off when he had the chance. He turned and looked at the minivan full of money that sat waiting for him, its engine purring like an eager lover.

He walked over and pushed the button to raise the door, again expecting a hail of bullets that didn't come. He drove down the drive and raced away from the house. Near the end of the street he slammed on the brakes and threw the van into reverse.

Grimacing as he turned his head, he drove in reverse back down the street until he was beside the SUV he had left parked there. He got out and grabbed the bags from the backseat and tossed them into the minivan before once more racing away from this place.

Friday July 1, 2011

7:33 PM

Tom "Bear" Burton drove slowly while he worked on devising some plan that did not include spending the rest of his days in a maximum security prison while awaiting an appointment with the electric chair.

He pulled up to the curb in front of the apartment complex where he had been living and parked behind the rusty old pick-up that he had been driving for far too long. As he made his way up the walk toward his front door, it burst open.

His girlfriend raced out of the doorway in cutoff jean shorts and a tiny halter top that seemed to be losing the fight to contain her ample bosom. She held a plate of food in her hand. Her hair flew out in all directions like the mane of a lion as she flung the dish to the cement sidewalk.

"If you think you're gonna stay out and get drunk all day while I stay here and wait on your ass, you got another thing coming. I've had all your crap that I'm gonna take and this is it, asshole!"

He opened his mouth to speak and she wagged a finger in the air, "Oh no, you can save your sob story for someone who gives a shit. I'm tired of your loser ass and all your promises and excuses. So just get in that piece of shit truck and get the hell outta my face."

She paused to take a breath and a hint of a smile played at the corners of his mouth as he turned and began walking away.

She called out to him in a less threatening tone, "Why are you limping? Are you okay?"

He paused briefly without turning around and without answering and then he continued on his way. She caught up with him at the sidewalk, "Baby, are you alright?"

He turned and smiled, "Never been better."

She threw her arms around his shoulders and kissed him as he winced in pain. She stepped back and stared into his eyes, "Come inside and let me take care of you."

He grinned, "Go get your shoes on and grab your purse, we're going on a trip."

She stared back with a puzzled look on her face, "A trip? Where to?"

"Just get your things; we need to get a move on."

She kissed him gently and raced back up the walk as he watched her longingly. A few short minutes later they were on the highway and on their way.

THE END

CRIME WAVE by

ROBERT JAMES CARMACK

Author Biography

Robert James Carmack is a native of Akron, Ohio and the proud father of three. A single parent with only two children still at home, he works full time in manufacturing. The story takes place in Akron with some liberties taken in the telling. This is his third book and he hopes that you enjoy the story.

The author can be contacted by e-mail at rcarmack@neo.rr.com.